The Development Dimension

SMEs in Libya's Reconstruction

PREPARING FOR A POST-CONFLICT ECONOMY

OECD
BETTER POLICIES FOR BETTER LIVES

This work is published under the responsibility of the Secretary-General of the OECD. The opinions expressed and arguments employed herein do not necessarily reflect the official views of OECD member countries.

This document and any map included herein are without prejudice to the status of or sovereignty over any territory, to the delimitation of international frontiers and boundaries and to the name of any territory, city or area.

Please cite this publication as:
OECD (2016), *SMEs in Libya's Reconstruction: Preparing for a Post-Conflict Economy*, The Development Dimension, OECD Publishing, Paris.
http://dx.doi.org/10.1787/9789264264205-en

ISBN 978-92-64-26419-9 (print)
ISBN 978-92-64-26420-5 (PDF)

Series: The Development Dimension
ISSN 1990-1380 (print)
ISSN 1990-1372 (online)

The statistical data for Israel are supplied by and under the responsibility of the relevant Israeli authorities. The use of such data by the OECD is without prejudice to the status of the Golan Heights, East Jerusalem and Israeli settlements in the West Bank under the terms of international law.

Latvia was not an OECD member at the time of preparation of this publication. Accordingly, Latvia is not included in the area totals.

Photo credits: Cover © Clara/Shutterstock.com

Corrigenda to OECD publications may be found on line at: *www.oecd.org/about/publishing/corrigenda.htm*.

Foreword

This study is part of the project "SME Development Strategy for Libya", supported by the Middle East and North Africa (MENA) Transition Fund of the Deauville Partnership and executed by the Organisation for Economic Co-operation and Development (OECD). The overall objective of the project is to support the design and implementation of policies for small and medium sized enterprises (SMEs) and entrepreneurship as important actors in the recovery and long term stability and development of Libya. Given the resumption of violence in Libya in 2014, the project had to be adjusted and some activitities were put on hold. The publication of this study completes component 1 of the project.

The recent conflict has led to the complete disruption of the political system. Apart from the very regrettable violence, the situation has also critically affected economic activity, infrastructure and social cohesion. The most urgent need for the country is to address socio-political fragmentation, conflict and to strengthen the process of reconciliation and transition. The economic outlook is extremely worrisome, and immediate measures should be taken to address the cash crisis and resume oil production. Once those critical conditions have been met, Libya will need to put into place or to strengthen the institutions and policies necessary for longer term prosperity. The development of a dynamic private sector, in particular of SMEs and entrepreneurship will be essential for employment creation, productivity and more balanced economic diversification.

The report is intended to contribute to the implementation of policies in a post-conflict Libya to promote private sector development. It analyses the structural economic and framework conditions prevalent in Libya, highlights potential drivers of development and considers the role of SMEs and entrepreneurship promotion in driving post-conflict recovery. Based on international experience and practices, and considering the context of the country, the report identifies the necessary legal frameworks, institutions and policies for the promotion of SME and entrepreneurship.

The study is based on information obtained from the Libyan authorities, such as the Central Bank and Libya Enterprise, and from international sources, such as the World Bank, the International Monetary Fund (IMF), the World Economic Forum (WEF), and bilateral aid agencies. The OECD also conducted a survey and a series of workshops with government officials, representatives from the private sector and academia, and experts from international organisations. This process also helped to build capacity with Libyan stakeholders on SME development issues and related policy-making.

To take into account Libya's context, the analysis incorporates the Principles for Good International Engagement in Fragile States. Those "field-tested" principles aim to help national reformers build legitimate, effective and resilient state institutions, while recognising the development challenges of fragile states (social tensions, weak governance, limited administrative capacity, etc.). The principles were endorsed by OECD Development Assistance Committee (DAC) development ministers and heads of agencies at the 2007 OECD DAC High-Level Meeting.

This study was directed by Nicola Ehlermann and Carlos Conde, and it was prepared by Pilar Sanchez-Bella, Lois Stevenson, Fares Al Hussami, Florian Theus, Hanan El-Nuweisri, Aliae Sayah and Mariel Juárez Olvera. The team would like to acknowledge the contributions made by OECD colleagues, including Antonio Fanelli – as lead peer reviewer –, Sara Batmanglich, Hans Christiansen, Peter Davis, Jorge Gálvez Méndez, Klaus Hachmeier, Fianna Jurdant, Kenza Khachani, Paulo Magina, Marie Estelle Rey, Anita Richter and Rachel Scott. The study was reviewed by Tunisia and Italy, the two co-chairs of the SME Working Group within the OECD-MENA Competitiveness Programme. Namely, valuable comments were provided by Mr. Saddok Bejja (Director General, Direction Générale de la Promotion de PME, Tunisia), and Italy, through Ms. Maria Ludovica Agro (Director General for Industrial Policy and Competitiveness, Ministry of Economic Development, Italy) and Ms. Benedetta Francesconi (Head of Office for International Policies, Directorate general for industrial policy and SMEs, Ministry of Economic Development, Italy). The report benefitted from the review and approval of the Editorial Board chaired by Marcos Bonturi, Director of the Global Relations Secretariat. This report was prepared for publication by Vanessa Vallée and Grace Dunphy and was edited by Richard Venturi. It benefited from the assistance of William Graff, from the Middle East and Africa Division.

Table of contents

Figures

Tables

Boxes

Abbreviations and acronyms

ACINET	Arab Anti-Corruption and Integrity Network
AfDB	African Development Bank
ALMP	Active labour market programme
BEC	Benghazi Business Enterprise Centre
BDS	Business development support
CAEU	Council of Arab Economic Unity
COMESA	Common Market for Eastern and Southern Africa
CSO	Civil society organisation
DB	Doing Business
DfID	Department for International Development
DZD	Algerian dinar
EBRD	European Bank for Reconstruction and Development
EFC	Entrepreneurial framework condition
EPZ	Export processing zone
ESDF	Economic and Social Development Fund
EU	European Union
EUR	Euro
FDI	Foreign direct investment
FOB	Free on board
GAFTA	Greater Arab Free Trade Area
GAGS	Government Authority of Government Services
GCC	Gulf Cooperation Countries
GCI	Global Competitiveness Index
GDP	Gross domestic product
GEM	Global entrepreneurship monitor
GFICA	Global Foreign Direct Investment Country Attractiveness Index
GIA	General Information Authority

GIZ	German Corporation for International Co-operation (Deutsche Gesellschaft für Internationale Zusammenarbeit GmbH)
GVC	Global value chain
ICT	Information and communications technology
IIAG	Ibrahim Index of African Governance
ILO	International Labour Organization
IMF	International Monetary Fund
IPO	Initial public offering
IPR	Intellectual property rights
IPRI	International Property Rights Index
IRC	Industrial Research Center
IsDB	Islamic Development Bank
IT	Information technology
KDS	Korea Institute for Development Strategy
KOSGEB	Turkish Small and Medium Enterprises Development Organisation
LARST	Libyan Authority for Research, Science and Technology
LBC	Libyan Business Council
LEC	Libya Enterprise Centre
LEPC	Libyan Export Promotion Centre
LLIDF	Libyan Local Investment and Development Fund
LPI	Logistic performance index
LPRD	Libyan Programme for Reintegration and Development
LPSDI	Libyan Private Sector Development Institutions
LTA	Libyan Transparency Association
LWEE	Libya Women's Economic Empowerment
LYD	Libyan Dinar
MAD	Moroccan dirham
MEDA	Mennonite Economic Development Associates
MENA	Middle East and North Africa
MOBIN	MENA-OECD Business Integrity Network
MSME	Micro, small and medium enterprise
NA	Not available
NBTVE	Libyan Board for Technical and Vocational Education
NEDB	National Economic Development Board
NGO	Non-governmental organisation

NIS	National Innovation System
NPC	National Planning Council
OECD	Organisation for Economic Co-operation and Development
PIB	Privatisation and Investment Board
PPP	Public-private partnership
PSD	Private sector development
R&D	Research and development
RCA	Revealed comparative advantage
RIA	Regulatory impact assessment
SBA	Small Business Act (for Europe)
SDP	Supplier development programme
SEZ	Special economic zone
SFD	Social Fund for Development
SME	Small and medium enterprise
SOE	State-owned enterprise
SYB	Start your business
TL	Turkish lira
UAE	United Arab Emirates
UN	United Nations
UNCAC	United Nations Convention Against Corruption
UNCTAD	United Nations Conference on Trade and Development
UNDP	United Nations Development Programme
UNIDO	United Nations Industrial Development Organization
US	United States
USAID	United States Agency for International Development
USD	United States dollar
VAT	Value-added tax
VLW	Voice of Libyan Women
VSE	Very small enterprise
WEC	Women's Enterprise Centre
WEF	World Economic Forum
WJP	World Justice Project
WTO	World Trade Organization

Executive summary

Libya's private sector faces many constraints, hampering both its development and growth potential. The recent conflict has made the situation dire. This report analyses the structural economic and framework conditions affecting private sector development in Libya. It includes recommendations to support the survival and growth of SMEs, as they will play an important role for the stability and long-term development of the country. The private sector accounts for only about 5% of Libya's GDP. A full 95% of private enterprises are SMEs, often operating in the informal economy. They perform poorly when it comes to generating employment, productivity, competitiveness and value added.

The main economic constraints to growth dating from the pre-2011 system are dependence on oil revenues, the predominance of the public over the private sector and unemployment. Framework conditions are not favourable for private sector and SME development. Libyan entrepreneurs have to deal with burdensome regulations, complex administrative procedures, high levels of corruption and weak rule of law. The financial sector is small and underdeveloped. And although the level of educational attainment has improved significantly in the last decades, there is a mismatch between the skills needed by the private sector and those provided by the educational system.

At the same time, political events since 2011 have impacted the private sector in many ways. More than 77% of enterprises in Libya report having sustained a direct impact in the past five years of crisis. Not only does insecurity take a direct toll on businesses' daily operations, but uncertainty reduces the likelihood of long-term investments. On top of this, infrastructure has been destroyed, and there is no transparent regulatory structure.

Nevertheless, previous governments did undertake significant reforms. The government of Gaddafi launched a series of economic reforms to move towards a more open economy and to revive the private sector. Among others, in 2010 a major legal review took place resulting in the enactment of 22 new laws and amendment of additional legislation, making fundamental changes relating to commercial activities, customs, income tax, the stock market, labour regulations and land registration. After the 2011 revolution and before conflict re-erupted in 2014, a window of opportunity opened during which there was strong momentum for reform. Among other things, the government signed a trade agreement with the US and started negotiations with the EU; introduced a new single window for investment; approved a national strategy for innovation; and many initiatives were launched with the support of international organisations.

As a unity government is coming to power and institutions become fully operational again, the first step should be to reassess the situation and identify what elements are valid to build on. A strategic focus on SMEs constitutes a vital ingredient for developing the productive structure and diversifying Libya's economy. SMEs are particularly important since they are more likely than large enterprises to create jobs for marginalised members of the population, such as youth and women. In post-conflict states with a long history of state dominance and in transition to a market-driven and modern economy, the main avenue for diversification and job growth is through new entrepreneurial activity.

Promoting SMEs and entrepreneurship will be essential for Libya to develop a more dynamic private sector, create jobs and incomes and increase economic diversification and resilience once socio-political stability is re-established. In the short term, this will require policies to rebuild the fabric of SMEs. It will be critical to involve local private sector in the reconstruction efforts to rebuild the country once the conflict is over.

The study focuses on structural issues related to SME development while also taking into account the impact of the conflict in Libya. Chapter 1 begins by analysing how conflict and fragility affect future policy making and how private sector development can support recovery and stabilisation. Chapter 2 examines the SME landscape, its performance and priority sectors. Chapter 3 assesses the main framework conditions affecting private sector development. This includes conditions that affect all private enterprises, such as the macroeconomic environment, the educational system, the labour force, infrastructure, the development of financial markets and the system of innovation. It also includes conditions that particularly hinder SMEs, either because they act as entry barriers (e.g. trade restrictions, regulations, competition and foreign and domestic investment) or they directly affect a company's operations (e.g. the ease of doing business, tax and labour regulations, the rule of law and corruption).

Chapter 4 reviews Libya's SME policies, including the institutional setup and specific measures. Once the political situation is stabilised, this information will be particularly valuable in taking stock of what has been done and assessing what can be the priority actions and main gaps to address in a post-conflict scenario. Finally, Chapter 5 outlines recommendations to support SMEs, including the possibility of developing an SME strategy. Based on international experience and practices, and given the very particular reality of the country, this report identifies actors and actions to put in place a legal framework, institutions and policies for the promotion of SMEs and entrepreneurship.

Chapter 1

Libya's conflict and implications for private sector development

This chapter analyses the political context in Libya, briefly looking at the ongoing conflict and underlying dynamics. It discusses how conflict and fragility hampers private sector development, and vice versa, how supporting SMEs, entrepreneurship and the private sector as a whole can contribute to peace and stability. International actors should develop a conflict-sensitive approach and follow the principles for good international engagement in fragile states.

1.1. Libya's political context

Libya has great development potential: it has one of the largest oil reserves globally,[1] is close to the EU – the world's largest economic block – and boasts relatively high levels of education. With a population of 6.3 million inhabitants and a surface of 1 759 540 square kilometres, it is one of the least densely populated countries in the world.[2] The population is concentrated in the coastal cities, and society is divided into about 140 tribal groups and clans.

Between 1969 and 2011 Libya was ruled by President Muammar Gaddafi as a *Jamahiriya* (republic of the people). In 2011, the Arab Spring protests escalated into a full-scale conflict and eventually led to the overthrow of the government. The first free elections took place in 2012, giving way to a wave of optimism and hope. But events developed in a negative direction (Table 1.1). In 2014, violence erupted again and the country gradually sank into civil war. Libya was divided into two rival camps: the General National Congress in the west (Tripoli) backed by the Libya Dawn coalition; and the House of Representatives in the east (Tobruk) backed by General Khalifa Hiftar and Operation Dignity.

Table 1.1. **Major events during 2011-2016 in Libya**

Year	Major event
2011	• February – Anti-Gaddafi uprising and overthrow of the government. • July – The international Contact Group on Libya recognises the main opposition group, the National Transitional Council (NTC), as the legitimate government of Libya. • October – The NTC declares the liberation of Libya.
2012	• July – First free elections and formation of the General National Congress (GNC), which replaces the NTC. • September – Attack on US consulate in Benghazi.
2013	• April – The US and UK report that they are withdrawing diplomatic staff. • August – Petroleum Facilities Guard militia begins blockade of oil export terminals.
2014	• June – A new parliament chosen in elections marred by a low turn-out attributed to security fears and boycotts; Islamists suffer heavy defeat. Fighting breaks out between forces loyal to outgoing GNC and new parliament. • July – UN staff pull out, embassies shut, and foreigners evacuated as security situation deteriorates. Tripoli international airport is largely destroyed. Ansar al-Sharia seizes control of most of Benghazi. • October – Islamic State extremist militia seizes control of port of Derna in eastern Libya.
2015	• January – Libyan army and Tripoli-based militia alliance declare partial ceasefire after UN-sponsored talks in Geneva. • December – UN-brokered agreement reached to establish a unity government.
2016	• January – UN announces new, Tunisia-based interim government, but neither Tobruk nor Tripoli parliaments agree to recognise its authority. • March – New Government of National Accord (GNA) arrives in Tripoli by boat and sets up office in a naval base. • April – UN staff return to Tripoli. • July – The GNA moved from the naval base to their official offices.

In December 2015, the UN brokered an agreement leading to the creation of the Government of National Accord (GNA) and a Presidential Council. The Presidential Council, headed by Prime Minister Fayez Sarraj and composed of eight other members, arrived in Tripoli in March 2016 to set up the new government. But its legitimacy is still contested – mainly because the House of Representatives has not endorsed it yet – and it has little control over the territory. This leaves three rival governments competing for recognition and authority.

Even if the GNA succeeds in stabilising the country, acute damage has been done and the underlying dynamics will be difficult to resolve. The conflict has brought to the surface a lack of social cohesion between the numerous clans. In addition, there is a growing presence of extremists associated with the Islamic State, who have targeted oil fields and control parts of the country.

Since the central government fell apart in 2014, the role of local governments and militias has increased (Danvers, 2016). At the central level, three institutions that have continued to function remaining largely neutral: the Central Bank of Libya, the National Oil Corporation, and the Libyan Investment Authority. The Central Bank, thanks to a political agreement reached before the government split, has continued paying salaries to both sides.[3] Given the state is the main employer in the country, maintaining government salaries mitigates the toll of conflict on the population. But there is an acute cash crisis linked to the paralysis of the banking sector, rising inflation and an increasing informal sector (ECFR, 2016). Furthermore, as reserves are being depleted, the situation is not sustainable over the long term.

Conflict and unrest have shaken the economy and will have long lasting consequences. Oil production drastically decreased due to attacks and the dispute between the different governments over who controls hydrocarbon resources. In December 2012, Libya was producing 1.37 million barrels per day; three years later it reported production of only around 404 000 barrels per day.[4] The decrease in oil output coupled with lower international prices has significantly deteriorated Libya's macroeconomic position. Between 2008 and 2014, GDP per capita was cut by half. Infrastructure has been destroyed – restoring it would cost an estimated USD 200 billion over the next ten years – and lack of security impedes economic activity (World Bank, 2016). Access to basic services, including electricity, water, health care and education, is unreliable and deteriorating (UNDP, 2015).

For many decades, Libya's economy has been over-dependent on hydrocarbons, with the oil, gas and related sectors representing 65% of GDP, 95% of exports and 96% of budget revenues. This has made the economy extremely vulnerable to oil price fluctuations and distorted the labour market: before the 2011 revolution about 80% of the labour force was employed in the public sector, while total unemployment was 19% and youth unemployment was 48.7%.[5] Libya's youth bulge (26% of the population is under 15) makes job creation an utmost priority, yet the private sector remains underdeveloped and the oil sector only accounts for 2% of employment. Private sector development and economic diversification will be needed to absorb the influx of new labour force entrants.

Economic recovery will first of all require short-term measures. Most importantly, oil production must be secured and the financial system rendered operational. Libya counts on vast reserves that can help finance reconstruction efforts. However, the international community must mobilise to provide much-needed technical assistance given the existing capacity gaps. Post-conflict reconstruction efforts should be taken as an opportunity for the development of private sector in Libya, which will require active policy measures to enable local companies to participate.

Ongoing fragility in the country will continue to seriously affect efforts of economic recovery if underlying dynamics are not addressed. A critical issue still unresolved is the basic form of government regarding the level of centralisation. Deep regional tensions have been at the core of the conflict. A highly centralised government will not be sustainable in the future, but the level of de-centralisation and the mechanisms to implement it should be agreed on – including a mechanism to share oil revenues.

In the long term, the government should develop a comprehensive plan to promote private sector development and economic diversification. Moreover, it should improve framework conditions to allow for a more productive allocation of labour and capital flows to the non-resource private sector. Additional policies will be necessary to stimulate the private sector through promotion of enterprise creation and growth, critical to diversify economic activities away from oil. It will also be important to build on what exists. Previous governments have introduced legislation, institutions and programmes in recent years which could still be relevant. Any future efforts should start by assessing to what extent these are still in place.

1.2. Fragility in Libya and implications for private sector development

The ongoing conflict hinders private sector development in many ways. First of all, there is no transparent regulatory structure; rule of law is fragile; and services provided by the government are negligible. Secondly, insecurity takes a direct toll on daily operations of businesses since companies have fewer customers and less reliable employees because people are frightened for their personal security. The unrest is also disrupting oil extraction and export, which has implications both for local employees and government revenues. Thirdly, uncertainty makes it unlikely that business people will invest for the longer term. Firms and investors will focus on short-term activities and survival rather than on creating durable businesses that can grow and create wealth and employment over time. Fourthly, the impact of conflict on infrastructure causes serious problems for companies. Power and water supplies have been severely disrupted, which has an impact on production and trading; damaged roads and poor communications make the distribution of goods much harder; and companies constantly face the risk that their own premises might be damaged by violence and fighting. Finally, the turbulence of the past few years has seriously disrupted the education of an entire generation. Relevant skills and capabilities will be lacking well into the future, with a consequent impact on the ability of the private sector to find properly qualified staff.

Private sector development can contribute to stabilising the country and should be a government priority from early on (World Bank, 2011, p. xiii). It should be an integral part of wider peace building and conflict management processes (Davis, 2013). The link between low rates of economic growth and levels of wealth and a propensity for violence has been well documented (Collier and Hoeffler, 2004). Providing inclusive economic opportunities for the population is essential for sustainable stabilisation. High unemployment, which is expected to rise, leads to the underutilisation of human capital as well as inequalities, exclusion of vulnerable groups and unbalanced territorial development, which could trigger more social unrest in the country. Addressing the structural inequalities and labour market inefficiencies, diversifying the economy and empowering a larger and stronger private sector are key to resolving Libya's employment challenges. The private sector can also participate in reconstruction projects, including infrastructure such as bridges, roads, and power supplies destroyed during the conflict. It can provide education, healthcare, commercial value chains and banking.

SMEs are particularly important for economic recovery because of their potential to generate jobs generally, and particularly because they are more likely to employ vulnerable segments of the population such as women, youth and refugees or internally displaced people. In rural areas, they contribute to rural stability, poverty reduction and social inclusion.

Conversely, a private sector which does not abide by the rules of responsible business conduct and takes advantage of the many loopholes that exist in weak governance zones can have a very disruptive influence – be it through nurturing corruption, not coping with basic fiscal duties, or damaging the environment. Businesses need to integrate conflict-sensitive approaches and respect the "do no harm" principle. Helping host states in conflict or post-conflict situations strengthen their legal and enforcement frameworks for responsible conduct is thus particularly important.

Implementing reforms is more complex in a conflict-afflicted and fragile situation. Lessons learned from other countries reveal that a failure to focus on the economy and private sector can lead to continued instability. Support should start as early as possible. Recreating an environment where firms can start up and operate can contribute to early stabilisation, employment creation, poverty reduction, and spur long-term growth.

Considering experiences of countries in similar situations, a protracted reform agenda and implementation can be expected in Libya. As the difficult transition unfolds, the government should begin with short-term measures that can allow for the reactivation of the economy. International partners working in Libya should recognise the particularly severe development challenges linked to fragility and conflict, such as weak governance, limited administrative capacity, persistent social tensions, violence or the legacy of civil war.

Although economic diversification is an imperative, political stability and security are a necessary precondition. Achieving economic growth will have to go hand-in-hand with broader efforts of improving governance and transparency and strengthening equitable institutions. Comprehensive measures for private sector and SME development will require adequate and stable government institutions and take some time.

1.3. Principles for Good International Engagement in Fragile States

International projects in conflict-affected situations have to adapt their operating model. First of all, events on the ground will inevitably impede the regular development of planned activities. Second, conflict and fragility have devastating effects on a country's institutions, which also affects the context of any project. The OECD Libya SME Strategy Development project had to adapt to conditions on the ground as security conditions drastically worsened in 2014. Although activities were halted during this time, the project took the opportunity to focus on the diagnostic and take stock of existing institutions and policies related to SMEs and private sector development.

Many stakeholders from the international community were active in Libya before 2014. As political developments seem to give some room for optimism, countries and international organisations are getting ready to resume their work programmes. It is imperative that international actors co-ordinate and look for synergies to work together in the future. In order to help national reformers build legitimate, effective and resilient state institutions, international stakeholders should apply the Principles for Good International Engagement in Fragile States, endorsed by OECD DAC development ministers and heads of agencies at the 2007 OECD DAC High-Level Meeting.[6] The ten principles are:

1. Take context as the starting point
2. Ensure all activities do no harm
3. Focus on state-building as the central objective
4. Prioritise prevention
5. Recognise the links between political, security and development objectives
6. Promote non-discrimination as a basis for inclusive and stable societies
7. Align with local priorities in different ways in different contexts
8. Agree on practical co-ordination mechanisms between international actors
9. Act fast…but stay engaged long enough to give success a chance
10. Avoid pockets of exclusion ("aid orphans")

There is much uncertainty regarding the political context in Libya, including how successful the Government of National Accord will be, how the political agreement will impact institutions and their mandates, and whether the security situation will improve or not. All of these questions should be taken into account when working on SME policies in Libya. The first step for any intervention should be conducting a conflict sensitivity analysis to identify the stakeholders in place, the drivers of conflict and peace, and what impact the intervention could have. Given Libya's society is organised by clans, identifying these ties will be essential to mitigating potential risks. Some lessons learned can be drawn from other countries like Iraq (Box 1.1).

Box 1.1. Lessons learned working on Iraq's investment framework

The OECD has been working with the Government of Iraq between 2013-16 on "Improving the business and investment climate". During this time, the country has continued to be affected by fragility and conflict, including the attacks of the "Islamic State". Among other things, the OECD helped the Iraqi government revise the Investment Law and ratify the Convention on the Settlement of Investment Disputes (ICSID), which provides investors with a mechanism for dispute resolution.

In applying the Principles for Good International Engagement in Fragile States, the OECD Iraq Project developed the following "lessons learned":

- **"Do no harm"**: During the inception phase, the project conducted a conflict sensitivity and a stakeholder analysis to ensure that it followed the "do no harm" principle – i.e. that it should not add to existing political tensions in Iraq. These studies allowed the project to involve a wide and balanced representation of stakeholders in its activities and have increased its acceptance, ownership and thus impact.
- **Flexible approach**: To respond quickly to emerging or changing reform priorities of the Iraqi government, the project conducted bi-annual impact assessments of its activities to determine the suitability of its policy advice provisions and donor demands for tangible results.
- **Recognise multi-dimension objectives:** During the inception period, the team analysed how its activities related to the cross-cutting development issues of poverty reduction, gender mainstreaming and conflict sensitivity. To monitor and evaluate how these cross-cutting issues were integrated, the project defined certain targets and milestones. This approach created awareness and better understanding among stakeholders of how activities could contribute to stability and other, broader developmental goals of Iraq.
- **Project ownership:** The project built relationships with key stakeholders to gauge their priorities and take stock of what they expected from reform. It successfully ensured strong ownership through the project working group, which was inclusive and brought together high-level policy makers (e.g. the Prime Minister's Economic Advisor), representatives from ministries, civil society and the private sector. That inclusive approach, in turn, kept the project in regular contact with a diverse group of stakeholders who advised on activities and impact.
- **Strengthen intergovernmental and public-private dialogue**: The project engaged private sector stakeholders, which opened new, wider perspectives in discussing policies at the meetings. The project also included representatives of foreign firms to share their views, constraints and outlooks on investment in Iraq.

Libya's conflict will have long lasting consequences, particularly on institutions and governance structures. International partners should focus on capacity building in order to support the main institutions that have a role in economic policy in general – including the Central Bank, the ministries of finance, economy, industry and others – as well as those involved with policies to support SMEs and entrepreneurship, such as Libya Enterprise or the Regional Funds.

Notes

1. US Energy Information Administration. www.eia.gov/beta/international/?fips=LY.
2. http://data.worldbank.org/country/libya and http://siteresources.worldbank.org/INTPROSPECTS/Resources/334934-1199807908806/Libya.pdf.
3. The Central Bank has the ability to disburse funds for wages and salaries (Chapter 1); student scholarships abroad; oil and gas sector; electricity (chapter 3); and, essential subsidies (Chapter 4).
4. US Energy Information Administration. Production of Crude Oil including Lease Condensate, Libya, Annual. Ibid.
5. International Labour Organization, 2012.
6. Development Co-operation Directorate (DCD-DAC) and Global Relations Secretariat (GRS-MEA), OECD.

References

Collier, P., and A. Hoeffler (2004), "Greed and Grievance in Civil War", *Oxford Economic Papers*, Vol. 56(4): 587–595.

Danvers, William (2016), "Next Steps in Libya: Economic and Governance Stabilization in the Face of Political and Security Challenges", Center for American Progress, Washington, DC.

Davis, P. (2013), *Corporations, Global Governance and Post-Conflict Reconstruction,* Routledge, London.

ECFR (2016), *Intervening Better: Europe's Second Chance in Libya*, European Council on Foreign Relations, London.

Joeng, H-W. (2005), *Peace-building in Post-Conflict Societies,* Lynne Rienner Publishers, London.

Naudé, W. (2007), "Peace, Prosperity, and Pro-Growth Entrepreneurship", Discussion Paper No. 2007/02, UNI-WIDER, World Institute for Development Economics Research, United Nations University, Helsinki.

UNDP (2015), "Instability and Insecurity in Libya", U.N. Development Programme, https://www.humanitarianresponse.info/sites/www.humanitarianresponse.info/files/assessments/instability_and_insecurity_in_libya_final.pdf.

World Bank (2016), "The economic effects of war and peace", MENA Quarterly Economic Brief, World Bank, Washington, DC.

World Bank (2011), *World Development Report 2011: Conflict, Security and Development*, World Bank, Washington, DC.

Chapter 2

Libya's private sector and SME landscape

This chapter aims to analyse the private sector, Small and Medium Enterprises (SMEs) and entrepreneurship in Libya based on available data, but the current situation is likely to have significantly worsened due to the unrest since 2014. The chapter presents information on the size, structure and role of the SME sector in the economy and the level of entrepreneurial activity. It highlights the major challenges inhibiting development of the SME sector based on recent small-scale surveys. The evidence reveals a very low contribution of SMEs to the economy, a relatively weak level of entrepreneurship and poor performance of the SME sector in terms of employment generation, productivity, and competitiveness. Private sector enterprises and SMEs face many constraints that hamper their development and growth potential, which have become even more severe in recent years due to the political instability and worsening security situation. This includes access to resources and markets. Much of SME-related activity takes place in the informal economy, largely due to complex and costly business registration procedures, the absence of functioning registration and licensing systems in Libya's regions, and weaknesses in the legal, regulatory and administrative systems.

2.1. Libya's private sector

During the early years of the Gaddafi regime, private sector economic activity was virtually eliminated and the State came to dominate all activities in manufacturing, agriculture, retail trade, banking, insurance and major services, with state trading companies in charge of all industrial, manufacturing and agricultural imports (AfDB, 2011). Gradually, to counter the negative impact of external pressures on the Libyan economy (e.g. US sanctions in the 1980s, the collapse of oil prices and the Gulf War in 1990/91), the government launched a series of economic reforms to move towards a more open and liberal economy and to revive the role of the private sector. But the impact of these reforms was limited. Entrepreneurship did re-emerge but mostly in the form of small-scale activities in the services and craft sectors, which carried low risks and required little private investment. Many of the adopted laws were not implemented and private traders were reluctant to re-open their businesses due to economic uncertainties and political unpredictability.

In 2006, the National Economic Strategy recognised for the first time the critical role of private enterprises in creating wealth and prosperity in Libya, including as key policy goals strengthening the macroeconomic and microeconomic environments and creating the conditions for productivity and innovation (General Planning Council of Libya, 2006). However, over the next five years, little progress was made in stimulating the private sector and development of SMEs. Since the start of civil unrest in 2011, the fragile government and lack of security in the country have further impeded implementation of the necessary reforms. The economy is still largely driven by SOEs (state-owned enterprises), which are active in many sectors and probably crowd out private competition.

Consequently, the private sector in Libya is very small, accounting for only about 5.0% of GDP and about 14.0% of employment (4.0% to 6.0% of employed workers and about 8.6% of self-employed).[1] These are low contributions to the economy by any international standard. Private sector share of total value varies greatly, ranging from 90.0% in the trade sector to 10.0% in the finance sector (Figure 2.1). In sectors where the public sector is dominant, private enterprises suffer from unfair competition with public enterprises, which affects their productivity and growth prospects.

Figure 2.1. **Total output value of key sectors and private sector share, 2014**

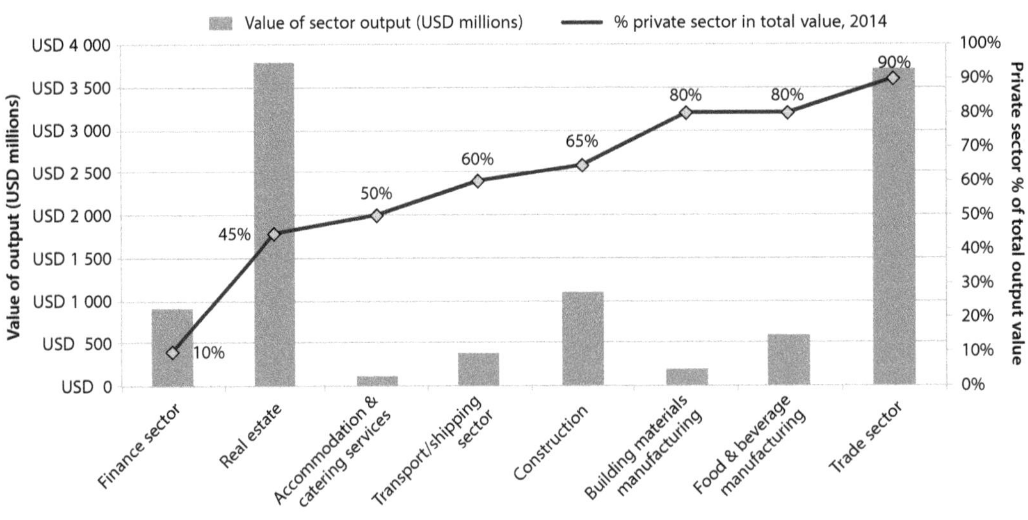

Note: Private sector shares based on World Bank calculations and estimates.

Source: Calice et al. (2015), *Simplified Enterprise Survey and Private Sector Mapping: Libya 2015.*

Government controlled sectors such as oil and gas, defence, health, education, social services, and electricity, gas and water supply accounted for over 85.0% of GDP in 2012.[2] Many other sectors are mostly controlled by public enterprises, although they are small contributors to GDP. These include transport, storage and telecommunications (3.0% of GDP), financial services (1.4%), and agriculture and fisheries (less than 1.0%).[3]

A small and underdeveloped manufacturing sector representing about 3.2% of GDP in 2012, a construction sector of less than 2.0% of GDP and a real estate sector of about 5.0% of GDP are comprised of a mix of public and private sector enterprises. The manufacturing sector is largely composed of state-controlled enterprises in heavy industry, with two strong private-enterprise driven sub-sectors – food processing and building materials production.

Most construction companies are large. At about 4% of GDP, wholesale and retail trade is the largest and most dynamic area of the private sector and comprises the greatest number of enterprises, which are mostly micro and small businesses (Calice et al., 2015). Other sectors where private enterprises are present, such as hotels and restaurants, private education and personal services, make a very small contribution to GDP but offer significant potential for future private sector growth.

2.2. SME definition and landscape

There is no officially accepted SME definition in Libya. Establishing one would be a first step to guide precise and consistent targeting of policies and programmes. In 2006, the General Planning Council (GPC) proposed defining small enterprises as those employing not more than 25 workers and having invested capital of not more than LYD 2.5 million (EUR 1.6 million) and medium enterprises as having 26-50 workers with invested capital of between LYD 2.6 million and LYD 5 million (EUR 1.7 million and EUR 3.3 million).[4] However, this definition is not applied by all government entities. Also, this definition may be too narrow.

First, it does not include a definition for micro-enterprises, which are commonly defined as having fewer than five or ten workers and tends to include most start-ups (Kushnir, 2010). This is an important oversight because micro-enterprises are subject to more severe market failures that differentiate them from SMEs. Second, the employment thresholds are low, particularly for medium enterprises, which in most countries' definitions are capped at 249 employees, as with the European Union's (EC, 2006). That said, some countries may cap them at as few as 100 employees or on the other hand at a substantially greater number as in the United States, which caps them at 499 employees. In addition, further consideration should be given to using annual turnover and/or balance sheet assets rather than invested capital as a defining criterion as the former are better indicators of the scale of a firm's operations.[5]

Globally, the SME sector contributes significantly to job creation and inclusive growth. In developed countries, SMEs account for as much as 50% of GDP and an even higher share of total employment (Ayyagari et al., 2003). This is not the case in Libya, where SMEs are estimated to contribute 5% to GDP.[6] While there is no official data available on the contribution to employment, a reasonable assumption based on other data is that SME's account for 11% of total employment.[7] Relative to other countries, this indicates much untapped growth potential for SME development in Libya.

There is no official data on the number or size of SMEs in Libya. The 2006 Business Census reported a total of 117 828 enterprises (Table 2.1), excluding the agricultural sector.

According to the census, the average number of workers per enterprise is 2.5, meaning that most firms are micro-enterprises, even in the manufacturing sector. The average enterprise size is much smaller in Libya than in comparable countries: an average of 4.4 workers in Jordan;[8] 12.3 workers in Tunisia (INS, 2012) and 6.2 workers across EU countries (ECORYS, 2012).

Table 2.1. **2006 Business Census results by broad economic sectors**

2006 Business Census	Hotels		Trade/ commerce		Services		Manufacturing		Row totals	
Number of enterprises	241	*0.2%*	83 298	*70.7%*	17 539	*14.9%*	16 750	*14.2%*	117 828	*100%*
Number of workers	8 360	*2.9%*	177 641	*61.5%*	61 022	*21.1%*	42 017	*14.5%*	289 040	*100%*
Of which, non-Libyan			36 986	*45.5%*	12 118	*15.0%*	32 044	*39.5%*	81 148	*100%*
Average workers per enterprise	*34.7*		*2.1*		*3.5*		*2.5*		*2.5*	
Sales (000 LYD)	149 621	*2.9%*	3 500 560	*68.7%*	696 362	*13.7%*	749 358	*14.7%*	5 095 901	*100%*
Sales per worker (LYD)	*17 897*		*19 705*		*11 411*		*17 835*		*17 630*	
Value-added (000 LYD)	105 169	*2.8%*	2 778 119	*74.0%*	464 984	*12.4%*	406 750	*10.8%*	3 755 022	*100%*
Value-added per worker (LYD)	*12 580*		*15 638*		*7 620*		*9 680*		*12 991*	

Source: Libyan Bureau of Statistics, 2006 (reported in World Bank, 2011: 8).

A full 80% of SMEs are privately owned by individuals, with 16% operating as corporations, 3% as family-owned businesses and 1% in other structures (AfDB, 2010).[9] However, many of the family-owned enterprises are small conglomerates owning a number of businesses, which in some cases leads to market dominance.

The food and beverages industry is the largest non-oil and gas sector both in terms of the number of firms and employees. The SME manufacturing sector is dominated by the production of food and wood products and metal for construction, with some small firms also engaged in the production of clothing, ceramics and bricks, grain milling and publication goods. Several fields of activity and opportunity are underdeveloped, with scope for expanding SME activities likely in the glass and leather goods industries, fisheries, consumer goods and tourism, as well as in the services sector. Given the right framework conditions and incentives, there is considerable room for diversification and growth in these fields. Linking small firms to the supply and value chains of larger National and Multinational Enterprises (MNEs) and developing higher-technology industrial clusters are other areas worthy of investigation (AfDB, 2010).

2.3. SME performance

There is limited data regarding the growth and performance of the Libyan SME sector. There is no statistical profile of the SME sector which tracks growth trends in the number of SMEs and their employment contribution on annual basis or the sector's dynamics (e.g. annual start-up and exit rates and net job creation). Neither are there studies of SMEs' performance that would provide an indication of the factors leading to higher value contributions of certain SMEs versus others.

However, the limited existing evidence indicates that SMEs in Libya perform with low levels of productivity, competitiveness and value added. Many Libyan SMEs are sub-scale, lack capital and do not have the capacity for sophistication in management and marketing. Monitor Group (now Monitor Deloitte) surveys found that 80% of SMEs employed fewer than five workers and 70% had annual sales of less than LYD 50 000. According to the surveys, a large percentage of business owners were "reluctant entrepreneurs", who would either prefer to be working in a government job or started a business because they could not find employment in the public sector (Monitor Group, 2006: 47). Libyan enterprises are characterised by a lack of sophistication in production processes, a limited customer and marketing orientation, low company spending on R&D, insufficient employee training, lack of access to international markets and inadequate attention to quality and efficiency. These all translate into Libya's poor performance relative to regional and global peers (General Planning Council of Libya, 2006; Monitor Group, 2006). In order to drive productivity and employment growth and innovation in the SME sector, Libya needs to improve the level of sophistication of Libyan SMEs by raising the management capability of SME owners.

The World Bank investment climate surveyed 244 Libyan firms in 2009, analysing their levels of productivity (reported in World Bank, 2011). Results showed that those which currently had a loan were less productive than firms without a loan. This seems to indicate that the financial system was not efficiently allocating credit to the most productive firms. Firms that received more regulatory attention – measured by the number of inspections by tax and quality control officials – were performing relatively better. This could either mean that inspections were causing firms to be more productive or that more productive and profitable firms were the focus of greater regulatory attention. Firms that innovated through new products or production processes were more productive. This suggests that policies to encourage innovation would enhance productivity, including eliminating unnecessary costs imposed by the investment climate, upgrading technology, reducing barriers to domestic and international competition and stimulating foreign investment and exports.

Since the 2011 revolution the destruction of infrastructure has further increased transaction costs for SMEs and decreased their productivity and competitiveness even more. A sharp fall in production capacity due to shortages in the supply of imported raw materials and goods, transport-related supply chain disruptions, loss of foreign workers and workplace security issues has also resulted in reduced revenues (Calice et al., 2015).

2.4. Regional and local variations

SMEs are unevenly distributed across Libya's regions. Business activity is concentrated in three main cities: Tripoli, Benghazi and Misrata, with most small-scale manufacturing concentrated in Benghazi, Jebel Akhdar and Al-Marqab (AfDB, 2010). External reports indicate that about 46% of SMEs are located in the northwestern Libya and about 36% in the northeast. This may simply reflect the distribution of the population since two-thirds are clustered in the northern parts of the country along the Mediterranean coast, with most of the population living in the major urban areas around Tripoli and Benghazi. There is also some evidence of different productivity levels based on the location. The World Bank's investment climate survey found that firms located in Tripoli were more productive than firms in other Libyan locations, hinting at the positive agglomeration effects, better infrastructure and social service investments.

The interior and southern regions of the country are less developed and likely to have a lower density of SMEs, a higher proportion of micro-scale enterprises and higher levels of informality. Less developed infrastructure, fewer economic opportunities and a lack of availability of business support services could potentially explain the lower level of SME performance in the interior and the south. There are also sector differences by region, with the agricultural sector being more dominant in rural areas, although agriculturally-productive regions are also located in the coastal plains near Tripoli in Jifarah and Jebal Al Akhdar in the eastern part of the country, as well as Sabha in the south.

There are also significant differences between the SME makeup of the three major cities. Tripoli is the political, banking, financial and commercial centre and one of the leading trade and manufacturing cities. Access to imported materials, availability of public utility services and a relatively high concentration of skilled labour are largely responsible for the concentration of trade, commerce and public support services. The SME sector, although small, is relatively diversified and plays a key role in the retail and small-scale manufacturing sectors.

Benghazi's economy is driven largely by a partly privatised SOE and other large firms. As such, it is not very diversified and private sector activity is weak. The Privatisation and Investment Board (PIB) invested in large tourism facilities to stimulate opportunities for employment, which could potentially create demand for new businesses to provide supplier and complementary tourism-related services (Altai Consulting, 2013). The destruction of infrastructure in Benghazi during and after the revolution has negatively affected the production capacity and market access of SMEs. From 2013 to 2014, over a third of businesses in the area reported physical damage to their premises, almost half moved their offices and 86% reported sales decreases, resulting in an average decline of 57% in revenue growth, the largest reported declines of any region (Calice et al., 2015).

Misrata, on the other hand, historically depended less on government jobs than Tripoli or Benghazi, although it is home to a number of large and small state-owned manufacturing facilities. Over time, it developed the reputation for being an industrial base, as well as for having a stronger private sector and more vibrant level of entrepreneurial activity than Benghazi, including a prevalence of large family businesses with a broad range of interests (Altai Consulting, 2013). The presence of a free zone in Misrata has also contributed to attracting foreign and domestic investment and enterprise activity.

Regional development is a major policy concern. In 2014, the government started working on an investment plan for Libya, examining the advantages and inherent potential of each region at the commercial and tourist levels with the aim of attracting investors.[10] The plan hoped to invite the private sector to participate in developing projects in every major city, with the state playing the role of the driving force and catalyst for guiding private sector investments in a certain direction, based on an analysis of what should be the main focus of each area or city.

2.5. Entrepreneurial activity levels

Low levels of entrepreneurial activity and high discontinuance rate

The culture of self-employment and private initiative was almost non-existent in Libya for decades. Entrepreneurial levels are still very low, as reflected by the Global Entrepreneurship Monitor (GEM), and the current situation can be expected to have worsened significantly with the recent conflict.[11] Out of the 67 GEM countries measured in 2013, Libya ranked 23 on the level of nascent entrepreneurial activity, 32 in terms of new business ownership and 63 with regard to established business ownership. Out of the adult population (18-64), 6.6% were trying to start a new business (nascent entrepreneurs), 4.7% owned a young business and only 3.4% owned an established business of more than 42 months, well below average for factor-driven economies (Amorós and Bosma, 2014) (Figure 2.2).[12] The gap with factor-driven economies is particularly large for the cohort of established business owners – 3.4% of Libyans versus 13.3% of the adult population in factor-driven economies.

Figure 2.2. **Entrepreneurial activity rates in Libya compared to factor-driven economies, GEM 2013**

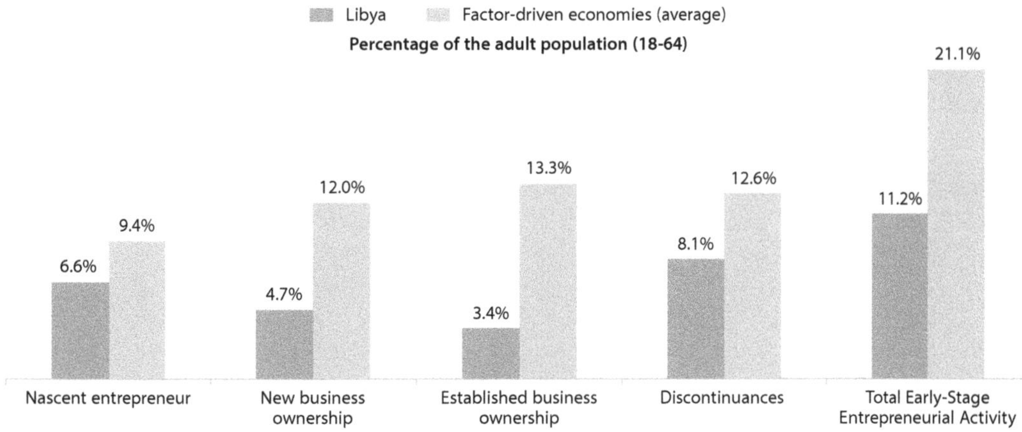

Note: The 2013 GEM-cycle included 13 factor-driven economies.

Source: Data extracted from the GEM 2013 Global Report (Amorós and Bosma, 2014: 30).

GEM data show that the base of existing business owners in Libya is very weak – only 8% of adults own a new or established business, compared to an average of 25% in factor-driven economies. The rate of nascent entrepreneurial activity is also comparatively low, although at the national level it is higher than the new business owner rate. Entrepreneurial activity is a recent phenomenon in Libya:[13] over three-quarters of adults engaging in an entrepreneurial activity had done so after January 2010 (nascent entrepreneurs plus new business owners)[14] and 58% of these were nascent entrepreneurs who had only been trying to start a new business after mid-2012.[15] Only 23% of all the adults involved in any entrepreneurial activity had been doing so for a period of over three and a half years.

The highest early-stage entrepreneurial activity rate is among the 18-24 age group, which suggests that young people are slightly more likely to develop their own business than other older age groups (Figure 2.3). In most countries measured by GEM, the highest early-stage entrepreneurial rate is generally among the 25-34 age group. Early-stage entrepreneurial activity rates in Libya increase with the level of education and higher income, which is common across GEM countries. These results suggest potential demographic targets for fostering the development of entrepreneurial skills and capacities.

The rate of entrepreneur discontinuances is 8.1%, which is also high relative to the other entrepreneurial activity rates and compared to other countries measured by GEM – only seven have higher rates.[16] In fact, there were more adults disengaging from a business than those trying to start a new one. So for every 10 adults trying to get a new business started, 12.3 adults were disengaging from an entrepreneurial venture. Entrepreneurs generally discontinue a business activity if it is not making a profit or they have difficulty getting financing. In the case of Libya, other factors could also be at play, such as the political uncertainty, security issues, destruction of infrastructure and disrupted market access. If more entrepreneurs are disengaging from an existing business than trying to get a new one started, growth of the already low entrepreneurial base will be further eroded.

Figure 2.3. **Early-stage entrepreneurial rates by age, education and household income level, Libya 2013**

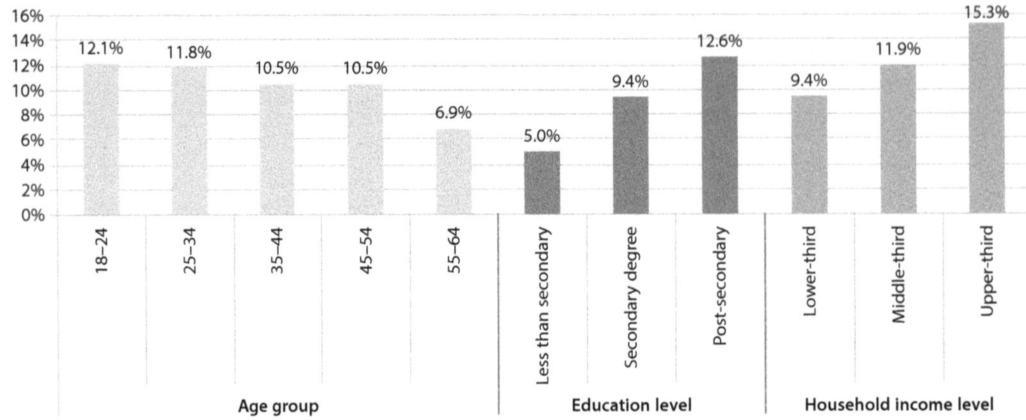

Source: 2013 GEM-Libya data.

Positive perception of entrepreneurship but low levels of self-confidence

Despite the relatively low levels of entrepreneurial activity, the adult population holds very favourable societal attitudes towards entrepreneurship. About 85% of adults see entrepreneurship as a good career choice and believe that entrepreneurs have a high status in society (Amorós and Bosma, 2014: 78). On the other hand, they have a low perception of the opportunities to start a business and their ability to start and run one, coupled with a relatively high fear of failure. Fewer than 60% of Libyan adults feel that they have the knowledge, skill and experience required to start and run a business, compared to an average of almost 70% of adults in other factor-driven economies. Just over half saw good opportunities for starting a business in the place where they live "in the next six months", compared to an average of over 60% of adults in factor-driven economies overall. And for a third of Libyans, fear of failure would prevent them from starting a business even if they did see good opportunities, which is slightly above the average in factor-driven economies.

These results suggest that efforts are needed to promote potential business opportunities among the population. Creating public awareness of burgeoning opportunities in strategic and growth sectors may have a stimulating effect on the rate of nascent entrepreneurship. However, the channelling of new businesses into strategic sectors would also have to be supported by other government policies to reduce the fear of failure that Libyans have. This could be done by creating a favourable environment for potential entrepreneurs to develop business ideas and transform them into reality, easing the entry of start-ups into new areas of opportunity and providing encouragement, entrepreneurial capacity building, business support and sources of finance.

Gender gaps in entrepreneurial activity

Gender equality is an important factor for economic development and growth (Booz & Company, 2012; OECD, 2012; IMF, 2013). The lack of resources and basic rights hampers women's potential to enter the labour market or to become entrepreneurs. This includes restrictions on mobility, property and inheritance rights, and access to credit. Losses in GDP per capita due to gender gaps in the labour market have been estimated as high as 27% in certain regions of the globe (IMF, 2013). Raising the female labour force participation rates to country-specific male levels would increase GDP by 5% in the United States, 12% in the United Arab Emirates and 34% in Egypt (Booz & Company, 2012). Better opportunities for women to earn and control income, and reducing the gender wage gap could contribute to broader economic development, while equal access to productive resources would raise the productivity of women-owned enterprises to yield considerable output gains (IMF, 2013).

Working-age women in Libya are ten times less likely to be employed as entrepreneurs than men. Only about 1.0% of employed women in 2012 were entrepreneurs, compared to 10.5% of employed men (Elgazzar et al., 2015).[17] Women account for about 4.2% of all the self-employed and employers, which is significantly lower than their share of the employed labour force (34.0%).[18] One reason for their low representation among entrepreneurs is the almost total absorption of working women into public sector jobs.[19] The 2013 GEM-Libya data reflect the gender gap in entrepreneurial activity rates, which is wider than in many other countries. Only 7.2% of adult females were early-stage entrepreneurs[20] versus 15.0% of adult males (Amorós and Bosma, 2014).

Libyan women represent an untapped source of entrepreneurial potential in the productive economy. They face specific challenges including the lack of technical and educational support, access to capital, opportunities to grow and the difficulties of balancing the time demands of family and work (VLW, 2012). Restricted access to economic resources is also a constraint for women's entrepreneurship in Libya. Over half of currently or formerly married women do not personally have financial savings, 64% do not own items of high value, such as a car or jewellery, and only 12% own land or an apartment (Abdul-Latif, 2013). This suggests that women are severely disadvantaged in terms of starting their own businesses and being able to pledge collateral for financing.

Closing the gender gap in entrepreneurship will require a mix of policies that seek to improve the business environment for all and explicitly target the entrepreneurial development of women (Piacentini, 2013).

2.6. The informal economy

Informality is present in all economies (Ayyagari et al., 2003; OECD, 2006).[21] But it tends to be smaller in countries with a business-friendly regulatory regime, competition-enhancing reforms, a comparatively light tax burden, secure property rights, less burdensome regulation of labour and a quality legal system (Pratap and Quintin, 2006). The incidence of informality also appears to decrease as firm size and the value of invested capital increase, although firms of all sizes may continue to operate informally when it proves to be too costly to do otherwise (Galal, 2004). Informal firms are deprived of the benefits of accessing formal loans, business development support services and supply chain contracts, which limits their growth potential.

In 2007, Libya's informal sector accounted for 30.9% of GDP,[22] which is not so high compared to other MENA countries (with the exception of Jordan and Syria, 17.2% and 16.5% respectively) but well above high-income countries, which average 16.6% of GDP (Schneider et al., 2010).[23] A large percentage of the SME sector is believed to be operating in the informal economy. The Libyan government estimated that up to a half of all workers were informal (Monitor Group, 2006: 37).[24] Many of these informal workers are graduates with basic education certificates or dropouts (GIZ, 2013).

Informal enterprises are generally involved in labour-intensive small-scale activities, operating with limited capital and rudimentary equipment and producing low-value products and services. Without upgrading and integrating into the formal economy, they are unlikely to become productive contributors to Libya's economic growth.

In the 2006 National Economic Strategy, the Libyan government included broad measures to address formalisation such as simplifying business registration and procedures to obtain permits and licences (General Planning Council of Libya, 2006). But little progress has been made. The government could conduct a study of impediments to formalisation and build on the experiences of a number of governments in the region that have implemented measures to bring informal enterprises into the formal economy (Box 2.1).

Box 2.1. Efforts of some MENA governments to increase formality among SMEs

Morocco

Based on an analysis of the informal sector in 2007, major incentives were introduced in the Finance Law 2011 to encourage micro-enterprises to become formal. Incentives included reducing the income tax rate from 30% to 15% for businesses with after tax income of up to MAD 3 million, with the condition they would create at least one job in each of the next three years, simplifying the system of value-added tax (VAT) payments and extending tax relief provisions for SMEs with a turnover below MAD 50 million (excluding VAT) for 2011 and 2012. The Ministry of Economy and Finance introduced a temporary amnesty for 2011 and 2012 to encourage informal enterprises to register for the professional tax (*patente*) as the first step in the transition to formal status. In 2011, 6 449 enterprises operating in the informal sector registered for it (World Bank, 2012).

The National Strategy for the Promotion of Very Small Enterprises (VSEs) aims to bring 73 000 informal VSEs annually into the formal system through major simplification of the regulatory and fiscal regime for VSEs, the establishment of support centres for VSEs in the governorates and provisions for upgrading and counselling/advisory support for VSEs (MAEG, 2011).

The most recent reform was the adoption of a regime for self-employed entrepreneurs. It is modelled on the French *auto-entrepreneur* scheme, initiated in 2008, which led to the registration of a large number of self-employed entrepreneurs. The aim is to significantly increase the number of registered self-employed individuals as a stepping stone for those aspiring to achieve SME status. The new regime, introduced in 2015, offers e-registration in the National Register of Self-Employed Entrepreneurs, exemptions from registration in the commercial register, simplified cash accounting requirements, certain tax exemptions and online declaration and payment of taxes.

Egypt

The Egyptian Small Enterprise Development Law (Law 141/2004) set a ceiling on the maximum time and cost required to register a micro and small enterprise and specified the establishment of one-stop shops in offices of the Social Fund for Development (SFD) in Egyptian governorates to facilitate the registration and licensing process and increase the level of enterprise formality.

Palestine

In 2008, the Palestinian Central Bureau of Statistics initiated a project to conduct an informal sector survey and add a module to its regular labour force surveys to capture data on informal employment and informal sector projects undertaken by unincorporated enterprises involved in market production. These surveys were intended to provide a comprehensive picture of the total size and composition of the informal sector in Palestine.

2.7. Challenges faced by Libyan SMEs

Libyan businesses surveyed for the *Global Competitiveness Report 2014-2015* identified the top six most problematic factors for doing business in Libya as: government instability, access to financing, an inadequately educated workforce, inefficient government bureaucracy, policy instability and corruption (Schwab, 2014: 248). These factors reflect the challenges to private sector enterprises in general and are likely to be even more severe for SMEs.

The cost of acquiring market information is high for SMEs and they have difficulty in securing or using the most developed technologies in their businesses, which makes them less competitive with larger enterprises. The smaller the enterprise, the harder it is to withstand demand shocks. Banks are reluctant lenders to the private sector in general and even more so to SMEs. Information asymmetries between creditors and clients are severe and are exacerbated by the lack of a Libyan credit bureau and other sources of credit information. The absence of collateral to secure bank loans due to the low property rights of Libyans in the past generation is also problematic.

SMEs' perceptions of the most severe constraints to their growth changed considerably from 2011 to 2014 (Figure 2.4). In 2011, the main challenges were access to land, regulatory policy uncertainty and access to finance (World Bank, 2011).[25] By 2014, political instability, macroeconomic uncertainty and corruption had become the top three most severe obstacles to developing their businesses (Calice et al., 2015).[26] Not surprisingly, Libyan businesses were experiencing more difficulty operating and greater growth challenges in 2014 than in 2011.

Figure 2.4. **Percentage of enterprises rating obstacles to operation and growth as "very severe" or "major"**

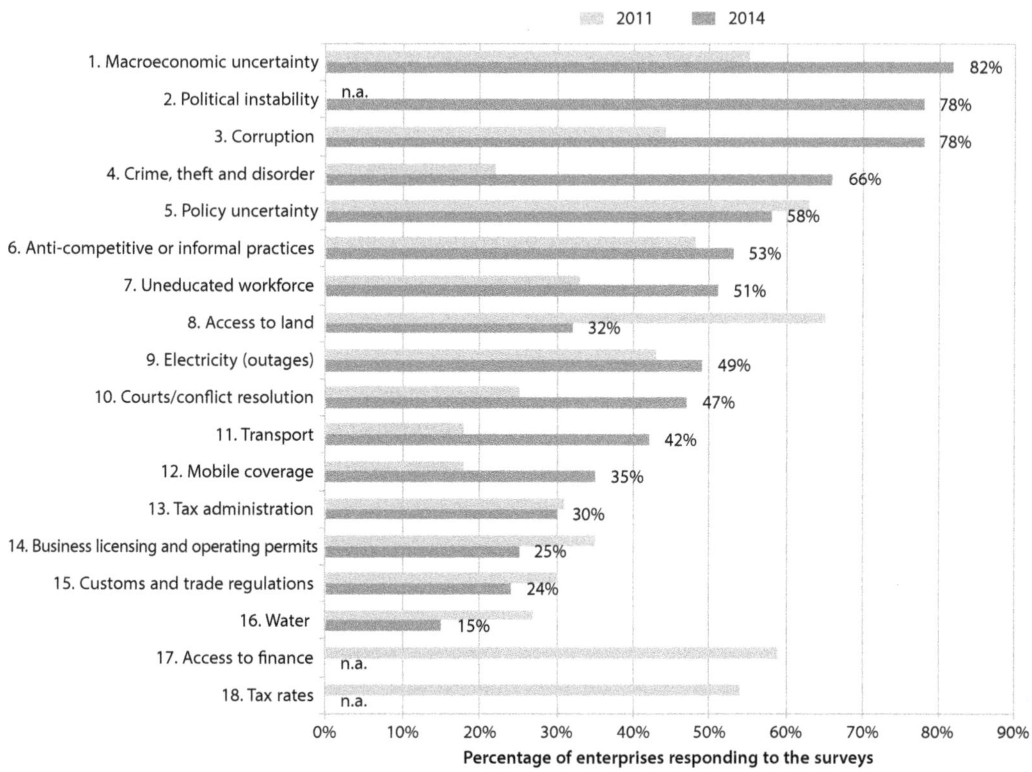

Notes: The survey covered 480 enterprises in 2011 and 457 enterprises in 2014. Access to financing and tax rates were not included in the 2014 survey. Political stability was not rated in the 2011 survey.

Source: Calice et al. (2015), Simplified Enterprise Survey and Private Sector Mapping, Libya 2015: 37.

Notes

1. Calculations based on data presented by L. Hargreaves, "Challenges and Opportunities in the Libyan Labour Market", 18 July 2012 (Altai Consulting). The breakdown of the workforce by employment type indicated a total of 1.4 million employed workers in the potential workforce of 2.1 million. The remainder were unemployed. Of the employed Libyans, 990 000 worked for the government, 175 000 worked for SOEs, 75 000 for private companies and 120 000 were self-employed.

2. Ministry of Planning data reported in Central Bank of Libya "Economic Bulletin for Q2-2014", Table 25. Includes: Mining & Quarrying & Other related activities, Mining & Quarrying (including Oil & Gas), Government, Defense & Mandatory Social, Electricity, Gas & Water and Manufacturing Industries.

3. The agriculture and fisheries sector has been largely driven by government-supported bodies and big projects, with privately-owned farms and agri-business activities limited in their capacity and having reduced economies of scale (Calice et al., 2015).

4. Conversion to EUR based on official exchange rate of LYD 1 = EUR 0.655358, 23 September 2015.

5. Registered or invested capital is rarely used in SME definitions (see Kushnir, 2010). Although registered capital is easily measurable on a national level, its relevance as a criterion for determining the size of an enterprise is highly questionable. It does not necessarily reflect the actual paid-in capital in any enterprise, and the scale of a firm's operations, such as sales and assets, are generally not a reflection of its registered capital.

6. Estimate of the Governor of the Central Bank of Libya.

7. This estimate includes 8.5% of self-employed workers and 2.5% of private sector wage workers. It assumes that SMEs account for half of private sector employment, which is about 4.0% to 6.0%. Data estimates based on L. Hargreaves, "Challenges and Opportunities in the Libyan Labour Market", Powerpoint slides, 18 July 2012 (Altai Consulting).

8. "Employees and Enterprises by Economic Activity and Size Group of Employment for Year 2011 for Private Sector", Jordan Department of Statistics (www.dos.gov.jo/).

9. Data compiled by the AfDB from Libyan national statistics 2007 (see Annex III of AfDB, 2010).

10. Information from Libyan officials at the OECD workshop on the SME Development Strategy for Libya, 25-26 September 2014 in Paris.

11. GEM research uses three indicators to measure the level of entrepreneurial activity in a country: the percentage of the adult population that is actively involved in trying to start a new business (nascent entrepreneurs); the percentage that actually owns a new business (less than 42 months old); and the percentage that owns an established business (more than 42 months old). The 2013 GEM study in Libya was conducted by the GEM-Libya National Team at the University of Benghazi, based on face-to-face interviews with 2 246 Libyan adults (aged 18-64) in July 2013, using the standardised Adult Population Survey used in all countries participating in GEM research.

12. Factor-driven economies, as defined by the World Economic Forum, compete on the basis of their factor endowments, primarily low-skilled labour and natural resources, with basic products or commodities as the main source of exports. They are highly sensitive to world economic cycles, commodity prices, and exchange rate fluctuations. The Forum classifies Libya as a factor-driven economy in transition to an efficiency-driven economy (Schwab, 2014).

13. The GEM-Libya surveys were conducted in July 2013, which was the reference point for gauging the length of time individuals had been involved in some phase of entrepreneurial activity.

14. The total percentage of entrepreneurs in the adult population was 14.7%. Early-stage entrepreneurs totalled 11.3% of the adult population, equivalent to 76.8% of all entrepreneurs.

15. The nascent entrepreneurs involved in trying to get a business started "in the past 12 months" made up for 6.6% of the 11.3% early-stage entrepreneurs, or 58.0%.

16. GEM defines a "discontinuance" as an adult reporting that, in the past year, they had "quit, sold or closed" a business they had previously owned and managed. "Business discontinuance" is not synonymous with "failure rate", as in some cases the business itself continues to operate under different ownership.

17. Elgazzar et al. (2015: 11), cited calculations based on the Libya Labour Force Survey 2012.

18. The female labour force participation rate in Libya was an estimated 34% in 2012, compared to the male labour force participation rate of 61% (Elgazzar et al., 2015: 8, based on 2012 Libya Labour Force Survey data). Although the female labour force participation rate is relatively high compared to other developing Arab states, many well-educated Libyan women are not participating in the formal economy.

19. According to "Libya in Figures 2008", 71.8% of employed women were working in the government, and another 3.2% in establishments belonging to the community (GIA, 2008: 14).

20. Nascent entrepreneurs or new business owners.

21. The informal sector can include non-registered enterprises that are not compliant with business and tax laws and regulations, as well as firms that are registered but evade some of their taxes and/or do not declare all of their workers for the payment of social charges.

22. Schneider et al. (2010: 4).

23. Informality in Libya was estimated to have averaged 33.7% between 1999 and 2007. Schneider et al. (2010: 4) define the shadow economy as "all market-based legal production of goods and services that are deliberately concealed from public authorities…to avoid payment of income, value added or other taxes; to avoid payment of social security contributions; to avoid having to meet certain labour market standards, such as minimum wages, maximum working hours, safety standards, etc., and to avoid complying with certain administrative procedures, such as completing statistical questionnaires or administrative forms".

24. The estimates were that 1.6 million workers were employed in the formal economy, and between 1.2 million and 1.6 million Libyans were employed in the informal economy, mainly in agriculture, retail trade, and construction sectors.

25. The 2011 survey covered 480 enterprises: 60% were small enterprises; 35% were medium enterprises; and 5% were large enterprises.

26. The 2014 survey covered 457 enterprises: 13% were micro-enterprises (less than 5 employees); 59% were small enterprises (5-19 workers); 23% were medium enterprises (20-99 workers); and 5% were large enterprises (100 or more workers).

References

Abdul-Latif, R. (2013), *Libya Status of Women Survey 2013*, International Foundation for Electoral Systems, Washington, DC.

AfDB (2010), "Technical Assistance for Small and Medium Enterprise Development: The Socialist People's Libyan Arab Jamahiriya", African Development Bank, Tunis.

Altai Consulting (2013), "Private Sector Research and Future Project Scoping in Misrata and Benghazi", prepared for the Department for International Development, Altai Consulting, Tripoli.

Amorós, J.E. and N. Bosma (2014), *Global Entrepreneurship Monitor 2013 Global Report*, Global Entrepreneurship Research Association, London.

Ayyagari, M., T. Beck and A. Demirgüc-Kunt (2003), "Small and Medium Enterprises across the Globe: A New Database", Policy Research Working Group Working Paper 3127, World Bank, Washington, DC.

Bennett, J. (2009), "Informal Firms in Developing Countries: Entrepreneurial Stepping Stone or Consolation Prize?" Research Paper No. 2009/19, March, UNI-WIDER World Institute for Development Economics Research, United Nations University, Helsinki.

Booz & Company (2012), *Empowering the Third Billion: Women and the World of Work in 2012*, Booz & Company, Abu Dhabi, Dubai, San Francisco and Stuttgart.

Calice, P., T. Benattia, A. Carriere and E. Davin (2015), *Simplified Enterprise Survey and Private Sector Mapping: Libya 2015*, World Bank Group, Washington, DC, http://documents.worldbank.org/curated/en/2015/09/25016718/simplified-enterprise-survey-private-sector-mapping-libya-2015.

EC (2006), "The new SME definition: User guide and model declaration", Enterprise and Industry Publications, European Commission, Brussels.

ECORYS (2012), "EU SMEs in 2012: at the crossroads – Annual report on small and medium-sized enterprises in the EU, 2011/12", ECORYS, Rotterdam.

Elgazzar, H. et al. (2015), *Labor Market Dynamics in Libya: Reintegration for Recovery*, World Bank Group, Washington, DC.

Elmansori, E. and L. Arthur (2014), "Obstacles to Innovation Faced by Small and Medium Enterprises (SMEs) in Libya", *International Journal of Innovation and Knowledge Management in Middle East & North Africa*, 3(2): 201–214.

GIA (General Information Authority) (2008), "Libya in Figures 2008", Great Socialist Peoples Libyan Arab Jamahiriya, Tripoli.

Galal, A. (2004), "The Economics of Formalization: Potential Winners and Losers from Business Formalization", Working Paper No. 95, The Egyptian Center for Economic Studies, Cairo.

General Planning Council of Libya (2006), "Libya at the Dawn of a New Era: Improving Competitiveness in the Global Economy", General Planning Council of Libya, Tripoli.

GIZ (Deutshe Gesellschaft für Internationale Zusammenarbeit GmbH) (2013), *Libya – Building the Future with Youth: Challenges for Education and Employability*, GIZ, Bonn.

GIZ (2009), *Libya – Building the Future with Youth: Challenges for Education and Employability*, GIZ, Bonn.

IMF (2013), "Women, Work, and the Economy: Macroeconomic Gains from Gender Equity", Strategy, Policy, and Review Department and Fiscal Affairs Department, International Monetary Fund, Washington, DC.

INS (2012), *Statistiques Issues du Répertoire National des Entreprises: Dynamique des entreprises du secteur privé durant la période de 1996 à 2011*, Institut National de la Statistique, Tunis.

KDS (Korea Institute for Development Strategy) (2010), "Establishment of SME-Oriented SME-Oriented TVET System to Support Public Sector Reform and Employment Promotion in Libya", Ministry of Strategy and Finance, Seoul.

Kushnir, K. (2010), "How Do Economies Define Micro, Small and Medium Enterprises (MSMEs)?" International Finance Corporation and World Bank, Washington, DC, www.ifc.org/msmecountryindicators.

LaPorta, R. and A. Shleifer (2008), "The Unofficial Economy and Economic Development", Working Paper 14520, December, National Bureau of Economic Research, Cambridge.

Levie, J. and E. Autio (2008), "A Theoretical grounding and test of the GEM model", *Small Business Economics*, 31: 225-263.

Levie, J. and E. Autio (2007), "Entrepreneurial Framework Conditions and National-Level Entrepreneurial Activity: Seven-Year Panel Study", Paper for the Third Global Entrepreneurship Research Conference, George Mason University, Washington, DC.

MAEG (Ministère chargée des Affaires Economiques et Générales) (2011), "*Stratégie Nationale de Promotion de la Très Petite Entreprise (TPE) : Rapport Final*", Rabat.

Monitor Group (2006), *National Economic Strategy: An Assessment of the Competitiveness of the Libyan Arab Jamahiriya*, General Planning Council of Libya, Tripoli.

Naudé, W. (2007), "Peace, Prosperity, and Pro-Growth Entrepreneurship", Discussion Paper No. 2007/02, UNI-WIDER, World Institute for Development Economics Research, United Nations University, Helsinki.

OECD (2015), "SME and entrepreneurship policy support in Libya: a diagnosis", OECD, Paris.

OECD (2014a), "SME Development Strategy Project for Libya: Consultative meeting for the diagnostic study - Meeting Summary", OECD, Paris.

OECD (2014b), "Protecting Investment in Arab Countries in Transition", DAF/INV(2014)11/REV1, OECD Publishing, Paris.

OECD (2013), "SME Development Strategy Project for Libya, Joint OECD/Libya Mission, Mission Report", MENA-OECD Investment Programme, OECD, Paris.

OECD (2012), *Closing the Gender Gap: Act Now*, OECD Publishing, Paris, http://dx.doi.org/10.1787/9789264179370-en.

OECD (2011), "Women's Economic Empowerment: Issues Paper", prepared by the DAC Network on Gender Equality (GENDERNET), OECD, Paris.

OECD (2006), *Promoting Pro-Poor Growth: Policy Guidance to Donors on Supporting Private Sector Development,* Development Co-operation Directorate Development Assistance Committee, OECD, Paris.

Piacentini, M. (2013), "Women Entrepreneurs in the OECD: Key Evidence and Policy Challenges", OECD Social, Employment and Migration Working Papers, No. 147, OECD Publishing, Paris.

Pickering, P.M. (2007), *Peace-building in the Balkans: The view from the Ground,* Cornell University Press, London and NY.

Pratap, S. and E. Quintin (2006), "The Informal Sector in Developing Countries: Outputs, Assets and Employment", Research Paper No. 2006/130, November, World Institute for Development Economics Research (UNU-WIDER), United Nations University, Helsinki.

Sandbakken, C. (2006), "The Limits to Democracy Posed by Oil Rentier States: The Cases of Algeria, Nigeria and Libya", in *Democratization,* Vol. 13(1): 135–139.

Stevenson, L. (2012), "SME Laws: Scoping Paper on International Practices", Prepared for the Jordan Enterprise Development Corporation. Unpublished.

Schneider, F., A. Buehn and C.E. Montenegro (2010), "Shadow Economies all over the World: New Estimates for 162 Countries from 1999 to 2007", Policy Research Working Paper No. 5356, World Bank, Washington, DC.

Schwab, K. (2014), *The Global Competitiveness Report 2014–2015,* World Economic Forum, Geneva.

VLW (Voice of Libyan Women) (2012), "National Policies on Ensuring the Economic Empowerment of Women in Libya", The Voice of Libyan Women, Zawia.

World Bank (2012), "Morocco – Country partnership strategy progress report for the period FY10-13", World Bank, Washington, DC., http://documents.worldbank.org/curated/en/2012/05/16276883/morocco-country-partnership-strategy-progress-report-period-fy10-13.

World Bank (2011), "Libya Investment Climate: Enhancing Private Sector Performance for Diversification and Employment", World Bank, Washington, DC. Unpublished.

Chapter 3

Framework conditions for private sector development in Libya

This chapter examines the framework conditions for private sector and SME development in Libya. It looks at the lack of economic diversification, macroeconomic conditions, infrastructure, labour market, financial market, the innovation system, the regulatory framework, corruption and the rule of law. Past governments have undertaken initiatives that have potential to ease private sector and SME development, but political instability and conflict have brought the reform agenda to a halt, affected the delivery of government services and curtailed implementation of laws and regulations.

3.1. Economic diversification

The oil, gas and related extractive sectors account for over 65% of Libya's Gross Domestic Product (GDP), over 95% of total export earnings and 96% of budget revenue (IMF, 2013). The oil and gas sectors in resource-dependent economies in general are significant providers of external income but lead to limited export diversification, a small share of manufacturing in GDP and a low degree of product sophistication. Natural resource wealth tends to heighten the likelihood that countries will experience negative economic and political pressures, exposing them to higher risk.

Recent events in Libya are a clear demonstration of these risks: the large external shocks from the collapse in oil prices and the ongoing internal conflict, which is disturbing the main oil fields and export terminals, are having significant consequences for its budget revenues and fiscal management.

These negative real income shocks can affect non-hydrocarbon economic growth in two ways. First, development of non-hydrocarbon sectors is mostly contingent on government spending. If government revenues decrease substantially, fewer budget resources are available to fund diversification efforts. Second, the volatility and unpredictability of oil prices, overvalued exchange rates, and political instability discourage investment in non-resource traded goods, which hinders the development of the Libyan private sector and overall economic diversification. This, in turn, creates a vicious circle leading to interrelated enduring macroeconomic volatility and stagnating economic diversification (Gelb, 2011; Calice et al., 2015).

Obstacles to diversification in resource-rich economies

Even under normal circumstances resource-rich economies face many difficulties in developing their non-resource sectors. Despite several attempts since the 1970s, Libya has seen little economic diversification away from hydrocarbons, only partly achieved in a few sub-sectors in the petrochemical industry. Since hydrocarbons are finite resources, Libyan policy makers should anticipate their depletion by developing a more sustainable and inclusive economic model. The diversification imperative is even more obvious in the current conflict-affected situation as resource dependency fuels social and political risks.

Diversification into sectors that are able to compete for productive resources like capital, labour and land involves a process of structural change that enables the reallocation of inputs to new and higher value-added activities. But one of the challenges resource-rich countries face are large labour productivity gaps between the resource sectors and the rest of the economy (McMillan and Rodrik, 2011). As a consequence, capital tends to flow either to the highly productive resource sector or to sectors created by the demand resulting from the disbursement of resource revenue, such as retail trade, construction or domestic services. The more pronounced this labour productivity gap, the harder it will be for an economy to accelerate structural transformation and for the non-resource private sector to develop, create jobs and raise overall productivity and income levels.

In Libya, labour productivity of the resource sector (i.e. mining and quarrying, including hydrocarbons) is more than ten times higher than average labour productivity, 30 times higher than in the manufacturing sector and 53 times more so than in the financial intermediation sector.[1] As a result, capital, including Foreign Direct Investment (FDI), tends to flow almost exclusively to the hydrocarbon and related sectors (Ianchovichina and Burger, 2013).

Some countries have been successful implementing diversification strategies. A new report by the IMF outlines policy recommendations for oil-exporting Arab countries (IMF 2016). Although political stability and security are a requirement for Libya to undertake any diversification efforts, it can look at other international experiences once it is ready. Some oil-exporting Arab economies have achieved certain level of diversification such as Bahrein – with the development of financial and banking services – or the UAE – with the development of commercial ship repair sector. In 2008, Morocco launched Plan Emergence to diversify its economy away from phosphates and agriculture. By 2014, exports from automobile, aeronautics and electronics – newly developed industries – surpassed exports from traditional sectors. Malaysia is another example of a country which managed to diversify away from a resource-based economy – primary commodities –, and it did so through a sequence of industrial master plans over a period of 25 years.

Non-diversified productive structure

Libya has a non-diversified productive structure with limited capabilities to produce competitive goods either in domestic or international markets. This is significant because the productive structure affects the path of development of new products and prospects for overall productivity growth (Hausmann et al., 2007; Hidalgo and Hausmann, 2009; Hausmann and Bustos, 2012). This principle also holds for regions within a country: those with more diversified and sophisticated production structures grow faster (Jarreau and Poncet, 2012) and are less fragile.

In 2010, the Libyan economy only exported about ten products with a revealed comparative advantage (RCA) relative to the rest of the world (Table 3.1).[2] While this level is comparable to other resource-dependent countries, such as Algeria, Iraq, or Kuwait, it is very low compared to more diversified economies, such as Turkey or Tunisia, which export

Table 3.1. **Composition and competitiveness of the Libyan export basket, 2010**

Product	% of Libyan exports	% of world exports	Revealed comparative advantage (RCA)*
Iron and steel powders	0.41	3.8	10.9
Crude petroleum	80.4	3.4	9.8
Petroleum gases	6.76	2.6	7.5
Acyclic hydrocarbons	0.58	1.3	3.8
Nitrogenous fertilizers	0.45	1.1	3.2
Other sulphurs	0.04	0.7	1.9
Gold, non-monetary	2.12	0.6	1.7
Liquefied hydrocarbons	1.61	0.6	1.6
Lubricating petroleum oils	6.41	0.5	1.5
Acyclic alcohols and derivatives	0.38	0.5	1.4
Iron/steel coils	0.23	0.3	0.8
Mineral tars	0.07	0.2	0.7
Inorganic bases and metallic oxides, hydroxides	0.06	0.2	0.5
Polyethylene	0.19	0.1	0.4

* Products with an RCA of 1 or more have an advantage in the global market. The higher the RCA, the higher the comparative advantage of the product.

Source: OECD staff calculations based on UN COMTRADE statistics.

more than 100 products with an RCA. At the same time, Libyan products are either in the petrochemical sectors (e.g. acyclic hydrocarbons, nitrogenous fertilizers, polyethylene and sulphurs), the metal industry or in food processing and tend to be exported by a large number of countries.[3] Additionally, they are highly energy-intensive products, subject to international price fluctuations, strongly subsidised and often produced by SOEs, which are protected by current regulations from the entry of other firms in these sectors. The private sector as a result has only a minor contribution to the export basket.

The Libyan productive structure is overspecialised in hydrocarbons, making it very difficult to expand into new product areas. The technology, capital, institutions and skills needed for the extraction of hydrocarbons are too specific to be used for branching productively into other sectors (Hidalgo et al., 2007). For example, the capabilities needed in the oil sector, such as drilling towers and petroleum engineers, are not easily transferable into other product areas, such as mobile telephony.

A way to visualise this challenge is with a product space map, which reflects the notion that the productive structure of countries evolves by spreading to "nearby" products in the product space (Hidalgo and Hausmann, 2009). The proximity between products in the product space reflects the similarity of the requisite capabilities that go into a product and shows the degree of connectedness between goods exported with an RCA and the rest of the productive structure. This is important because in their diversification efforts, countries tend to more easily "jump" into products that require capabilities similar to those required by the products they already export. If a new product is in close proximity to the current basket of goods, the private sector may be able to exploit existing capabilities by building on the markets, physical and human assets and institutions already acquired for pre-existing activities (Hidalgo et al., 2007).

Libya's product space map shows that most of the products with an RCA, even the non-hydrocarbon ones, are located at the periphery of the product space (Figure 3.1). Because Libya is specialised in peripheral products, with a concentration around the oil sector, redeployment of the set of acquired capabilities is more challenging as there are almost no sets of nearby products requiring similar capabilities, with the exception of petrochemicals and a few other products, such as metals. This represents a great challenge because it is rare to observe jumps across large distances in the product space (Hausmann et al., 2007;

Figure 3.1. **Libya's product space compared to Norway and the United Arab Emirates, 2014**

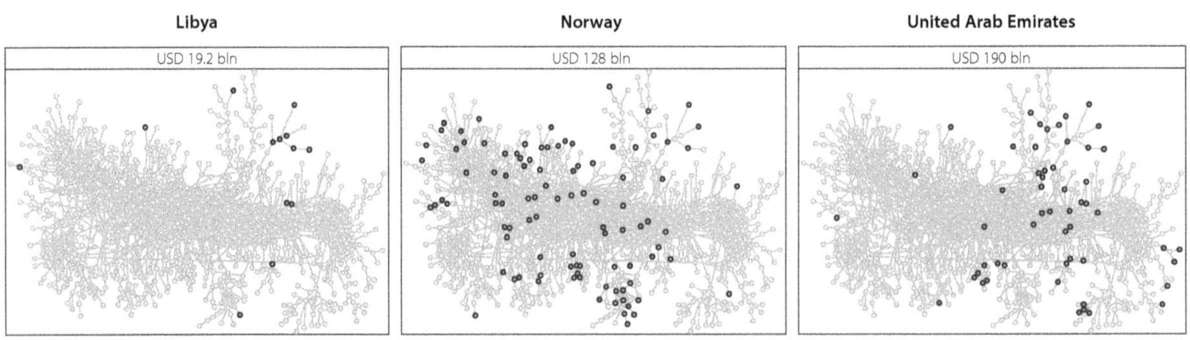

Note: Each node is a product, and its size determined by its share of total country exports. The opacity of a node indicates the degree to which the product is produced with an RCA. The product space map gets denser towards the centre and is sparse at the periphery. Many products group naturally into highly connected communities of products as they require similar capabilities (e.g. knowledge and factor inputs). The distance between the products represents the ease of "jumping" to another product.

Source: Hausmann et al. (2013), *The Atlas of Economic Complexity: Mapping Paths to Prosperity,* http://atlas.cid.harvard.edu/explore/product_space/export/are/all/show/2013/.

Hidalgo et al., 2007). Norway and the United Arab Emirates, both resource-rich countries, display a significantly larger number of products exported with a comparative advantage, and these are more widespread on the map, particularly in the case of Norway, which better facilitates the jumping to new products.

In addition to showing strong path dependence, a firm's production of new products is also place dependent. This originates from the proximity of available firms and local product-specific competencies to those needed to produce the new goods (Lo Turco and Maggioni, 2015). This implies that local competencies matter for firm innovation, and local disparities must be taken into account when exploring Libya's economic diversification challenges. The uneven economic geography calls for crucial action to improve the factor endowments in the less-performing regions. This will allow them to more equitably exploit product opportunities in sectors identified for diversification.

Potential sectors for development

Analysing the productive structure of the economy can reveal opportunities in new and unexplored sectors. The product space analysis makes it possible to plot sectors according to their level of economic complexity and their distance from current productive capabilities, i.e. their ease of "jumping" to another product within a same sector. It is then possible to identify preferred products which are high in complexity but not too far away from Libya's current productive knowledge.

Products are classified according to their RCA over the last two decades and sorted into four categories: 1) classical products, those which have demonstrated an RCA consistently over the long run; 2) declining products, those which previously demonstrated an RCA but no longer do so; 3) emerging champions, those which previously did not demonstrate an RCA higher than one but now do; and 4) marginal products, those which have never demonstrated an RCA higher than one. Overall, the results suggest that export in new product categories has been relatively weak, with the majority of products belonging to the marginal group, i.e. they were not exported with a revealed comparative advantage over the last two decades (Figure 3.2 and Table 3.2). The OECD conducted a stakeholder workshop in July 2015 to discuss potential sectors for diversification five sectors where identified as having the largest potential: building and construction materials; ICTs; energy and renewables; tourism, transit and logistics; and agri-business and fisheries (Annex 3.A1).

Libya has to find ways of stimulating higher value-added activities in non-natural resource sectors, particularly in tradeable goods and services. Producing new niche products where countries can attain comparative advantage involves a long and risky process of trial and error to test new markets. This process is vital to economic diversification. Regardless of whether or not an investment is successful, the social return of venturing into new product areas is substantial, especially when it leads to creation of a new industry. At the same time, more new product discovery contributes further to building and expanding a country's productive capabilities.

Figure 3.2. **The emerging champions of the Libyan economy: A revealed comparative advantage analysis of product community classifications**

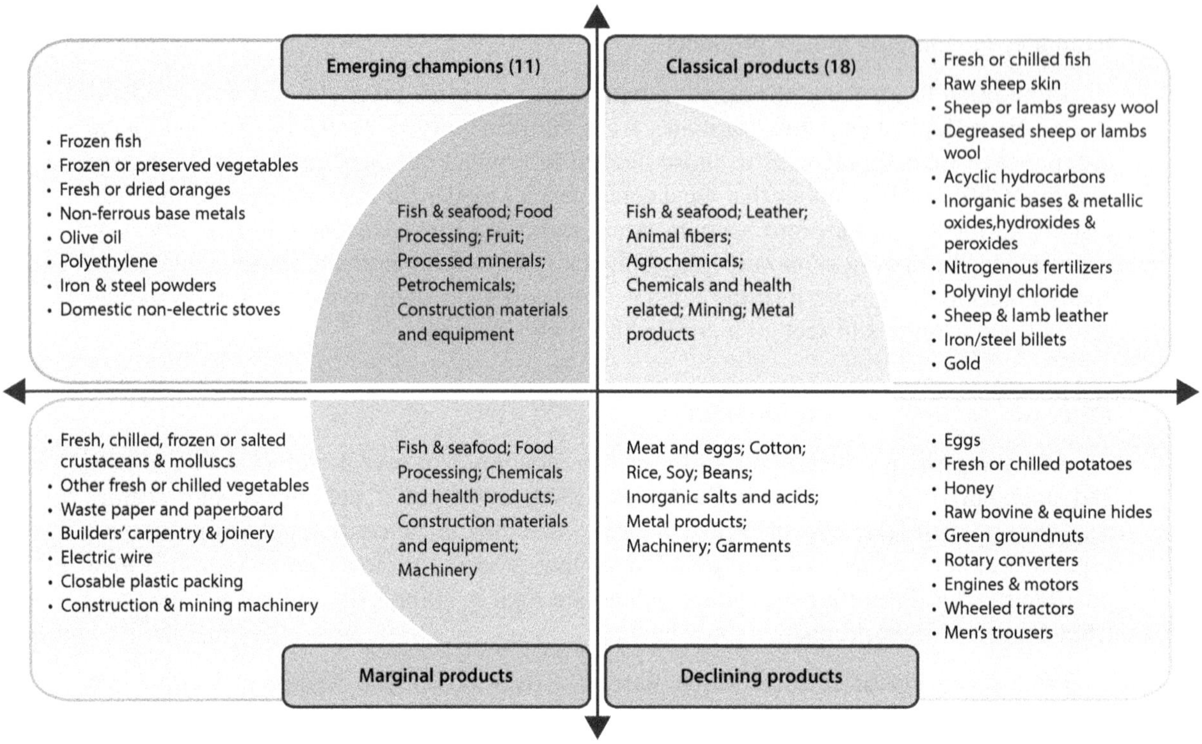

Note: The specific dynamics within and between industries within the product space are analysed, and Standard International Trade Classification (SITC) codes are used to determine the community structure. The rise and decline of specific industries over time can be determined in terms of network connectedness.

Source: Based on UN COMTRADE statistics and Hidalgo et al. (2007).

Table 3.2. **Potential opportunities for diversifying Libya's productive structure**

Product classifications	Features
Emerging champions: There is potential to develop products at the frontier of the economy's current productive capabilities and set a new production path.	• Only 11 products emerged over the last two decades as competitive in international markets. These are located in fish and seafood, construction materials and equipment, processed minerals, food processing, petrochemicals and fruit. Most of these products are resource-based or primary products, with a low degree of sophistication and marginal value-added, i.e. they undergo very little transformation and are mostly exported as raw products. Nevertheless, some products, particularly those in petrochemicals (polyethylene) and metal products (iron and steel powders), display relatively high levels of export sophistication, although even these undergo very little transformation. • Polyethylene has the largest export value among the emerging champions and witnessed an important surge in export levels at the beginning of the 1990s. It is followed by iron and steel powders, and non-ferrous base metals, which appear to have had only modest increase. Further analysis is needed to evaluate the world future demand for these products and the capacity of production of the Libyan economy.
Classical products (excluding hydrocarbons): They are crucial to guarantee some economic stability through relatively predictable revenues in foreign currencies. It is very important to maintain these sectors, particularly those where world demand is increasing.	• Over the last two decades, 18 products fell under this classification, mostly located in the sectors of fish and seafood, animal fibres, agrochemicals, chemicals, mining and metal products, with very low levels of export sophistication. The highest levels of product sophistication are in metals (iron and steel shapes), chemicals (nitrogenous fertilizers and acyclic hydrocarbons) and mining (inorganic bases and metallic oxides). • Gold contributes the most in terms of value to the export basket of classical products but has one of the lowest levels of product sophistication. Its unique productive capabilities cannot be readily used to produce other nearby products. In contrast, acyclic hydrocarbons and iron and steel shapes have both relatively high levels of exports and sophistication, implying that the productive capabilities used for these products could be used to make new products that require similar ones. It would be necessary to examine world demand for these products.

Table 3.2. **Potential opportunities for diversifying Libya's productive structure** *(continued)*

Product classifications	Features
Marginal products: They represent the bulk of the products exported in terms of number.	• These products are primarily located in the machinery sector, including construction and mining machinery. These products might be the result of the important oil industry in Libya and might only represent re-exports of previously imported products. Despite the fact that the machinery sector in general is located at the core of the product space, these products and the productive capabilities associated with their production (engineers, etc.) might be too specific to oil production. • Some of the marginal products are also located within similar sectors as emerging products, such as construction materials and equipment (iron and steel structures), food processing or chemicals and health products (polymerisation products). Although classified as marginal, these products should be observed very closely as they could also emerge in future years as competitive products of the Libyan economy. In particular, it may be relevant to explore more in depth the nature of the products in the machinery sector to better understand the scope of their potential role in the Libyan economic structure.
Declining products: These are products in which Libya has lost its revealed comparative advantage over the last two decades.	• They are located in sectors where international competition from countries with low labour costs has increased strongly over the last decades. They include meat and eggs, cotton, rice, soy beans, leather and, in particular, machinery and garments. • Some of the identified declining products have relatively high sophistication, such as metal products (iron and steel-related) but most are found in low-value added industries and, thus, it may not be relevant to defend them any longer in international markets.

3.2. Macroeconomic policies

Macroeconomic stability is fundamental to sustainable economic growth through the signalling effects given to investors. If there is macroeconomic instability and uncertainty, private investment is significantly and negatively influenced because unpredictability hampers resource allocation decisions, investment and growth. During periods of macroeconomic instability, entrepreneurs will operate on short-term investment horizons, choosing activities with quick returns rather than projects with longer-term investment returns, such as in manufacturing.

GDP volatility from oil price decrease and production disruptions

Following the lifting of United Nations sanctions in 2003, economic activity in Libya increased consistently for several years. From 2003-10, GDP grew at an annual average rate of 6.1%, even with the slowdown in growth during the global downturn in 2008 and 2009. The oil sector – favoured by a hike in global oil prices – contributed significantly to this economic expansion, fuelling revenues and growth. Even though growth rates were high, there was a relatively high degree of fluctuation in GDP growth trends between 2000 and 2010 (Figure 3.3). The 2011 revolution caused disruptions to oil production, which brought hydrocarbon exports almost to a halt and diminished GDP by 62%. Boosted by the resumption of oil production and exports, Libyan GDP recovered rapidly in 2012, growing by 104.4%, but persistent political instability and the incapacity of economic agents to conduct their daily operations, coupled with the fall in oil prices, led to negative growth rates in 2013, 2014 and into 2015.

The volatility in GDP has produced a significant drop in GDP per capita, declining from a high of USD 14 232 in 2008 to USD 6 570 in 2014 (Figure 3.4). This suggests less disposable income and lower consumer demand, as well as depressed investment possibilities. According to the World Economic Outlook forecasts, Libya should experience a steady increase in GDP starting in 2016 (IMF, 2015). However, this positive outlook will depend on the resumption of oil production and the ability of the private sector to operate efficiently, which are both contingent on an improved overall security situation.

Figure 3.3. **Level and rate of change of Libyan GDP, 2000-20**

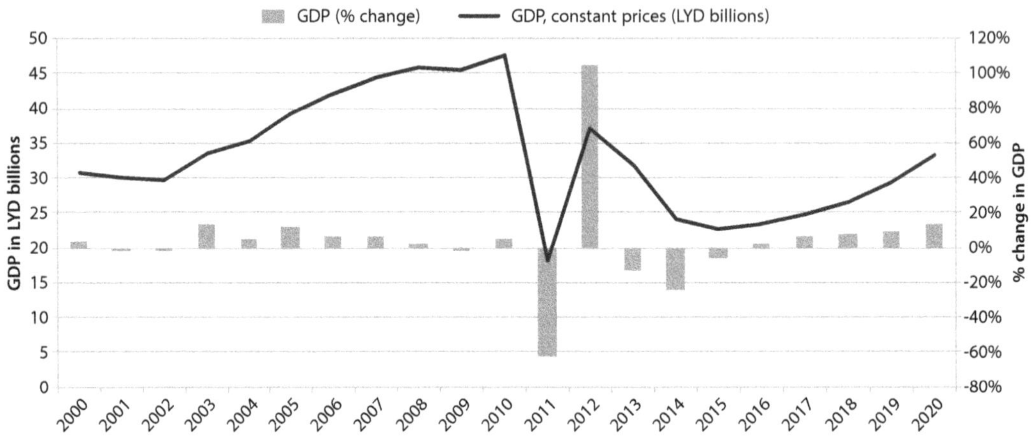

Note: IMF staff estimates for 2014-20.

Source: IMF World Economic Outlook Database, October 2015 edition, https://www.imf.org/external/pubs/ft/weo/2015/02/weodata/index.aspx.

Figure 3.4. **Libyan GDP per capita compared to GDP in constant prices, 2000-14**

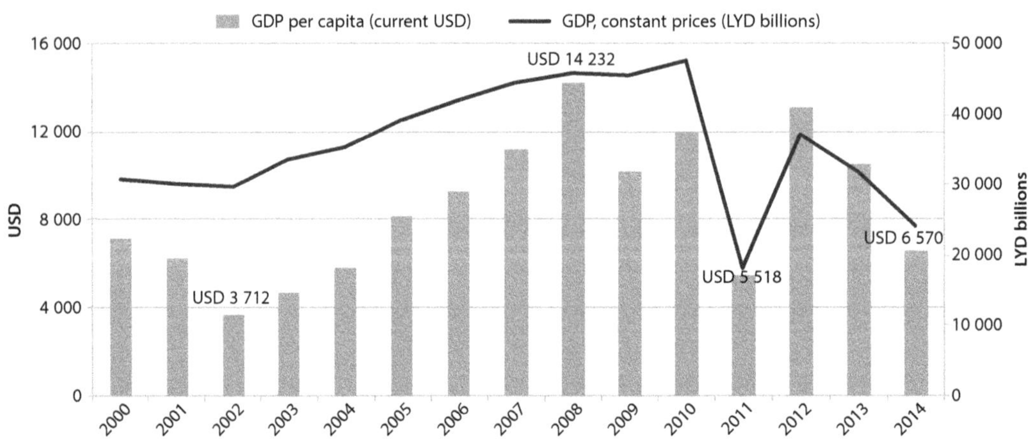

Sources: GDP in constant prices: IMF World Outlook Database, October 2015 edition; GDP per capita: World Development Indicators Database, World Bank, October 2015 edition.

Deteriorating fiscal position

Prior to the 2011 revolution, Libya had a strong fiscal position, with large reserves and significant revenues emanating from the oil sector. In recent years, this has been deteriorating due to fluctuations in oil production and depressed prices on world markets, with particularly large drops in oil revenues in 2011 and 2014 as a result of the worsening conflict (Figure 3.5).

Figure 3.5. **Government revenue from oil and non-oil sources, 2007-14**

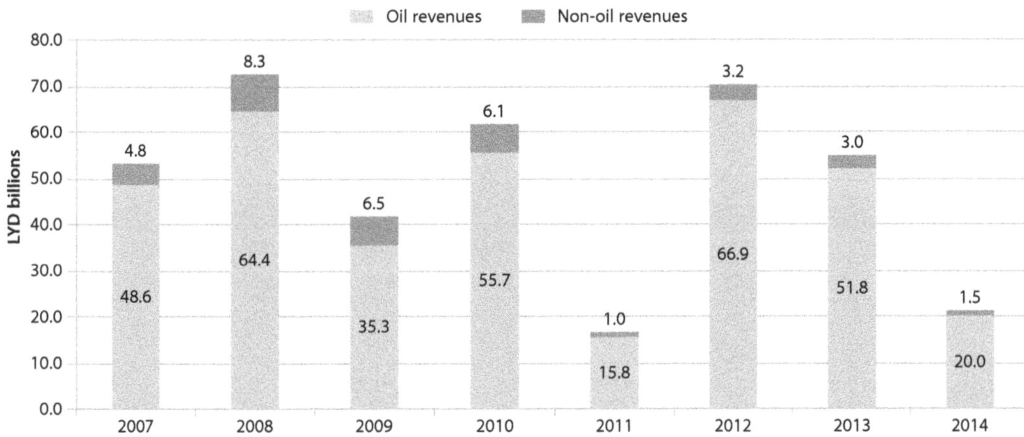

Source: Central Bank of Libya, "Economic Bulletin Q4-2014".

The non-oil revenue base is very small, amounting to only 7.0% of total budget revenue in 2014, the highest it has been since 2010. The volume of non-oil revenue in the public budget dropped dramatically in 2011, and slowly started recovering in 2012 and 2013 (Figure 3.6). Tax revenue makes up a minority of non-oil revenues, averaging about one-third of the total from 2007 to 2013. But it fell sharply in 2011 due to the lack of a functioning government. The already very narrow non-hydrocarbon tax base amounted to only 0.7% of GDP in 2012 and 2013, down from 2.5% of GDP in 2006 (AfDB/OECD/UNDP, 2015). Since 2011, income taxes from public sector employees and staff of foreign and state-owned enterprises have accounted for the vast majority of all taxes collected, largely due to deterioration of the tax administration, which has been able to maintain only limited central authority and co-ordination over tax collection (AfDB/OECD/UNDP, 2014). In addition, decades of high taxes and autocratic rule have created a culture of tax evasion.

Figure 3.6. **Composition of non-oil government revenues in the Libyan public budget, 2007-14**

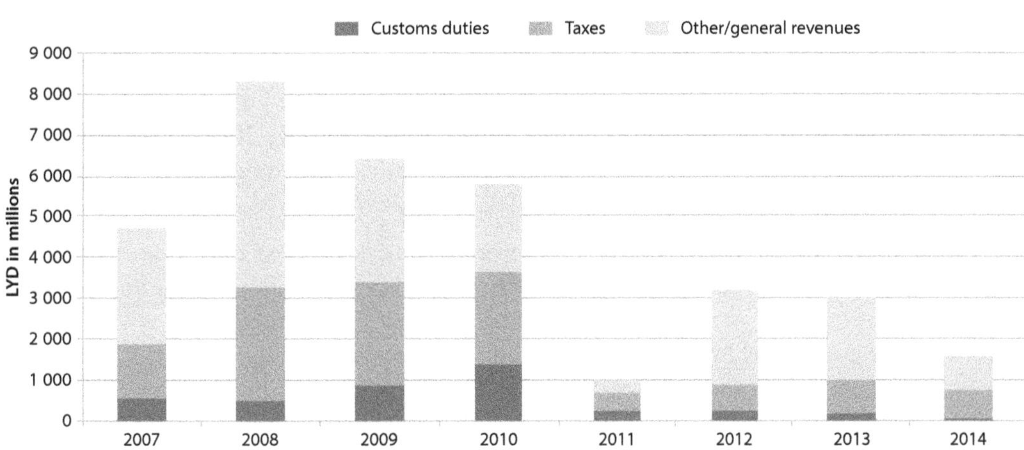

Source: Ministry of Finance, reported in Central Bank of Libya, "Economic Bulletin Q2-2015".

Before the 2011 conflict Libya had large budget and current account surpluses, but the recent disruptions in oil production and price shocks have resulted in lower exports and export revenues and led to sharp declines in the size of Libya's trade and current account balances (Table 3.3). This has caused a serious strain on the stability of revenue flows and Libya's fiscal position.

Table 3.3. **Current account balance, selected years**

	Percentage of GDP at current prices						
	2006	2011	2012	2013	2014 (e)	2015 (p)	2016 (p)
Trade balance	55.1	22.6	43.3	27.2	3.4	7.2	11.7
Exports of goods (f.o.b.)	78.4	54.9	74.5	62.7	58.2	59.3	59.3
Imports of goods (f.o.b.)	23.3	32.3	31.2	35.5	54.8	52.1	47.6
Services	-4.3	-12.6	-8.4	-9.9	-19.0	-18.8	-14.2
Factor income	-0.1	0.2	-2.4	-0.2	-0.2	0.5	0.6
Current transfers	0.6	-1.1	-3.4	-3.5	-7.6	-6.4	-4.6
Current account balance	51.4	9.1	29.1	13.6	-23.3	-17.5	-6.6

Note: Estimates (e) and projections (p) based on AfDB/OECD/UNDP calculations.
Source: AfDB/OECD/UNDP (2015), *Africa Economic Outlook 2015* (Libya, Table 4).

Libya ran a budget deficit of 15.9% of GDP in 2011, compared to a surplus of 11.5% of GDP in 2010. With the resumption of oil and gas production in 2012, the budget surplus increased, but in 2014 the government was forced to run a significant budget deficit estimated at 43.5% of GDP (LYD 22.8 billion), the highest ever recorded.[4] This was projected to improve in 2015 as the result of actions of the Central Bank of Libya to make drastic cuts in expenditures, mostly in public wages and subsidies (AfDB/OECD/UNDP, 2015). Even so, the World Bank was projecting the fiscal deficit to climb to over 55.0% of GDP in 2015 (Ianchovichina et al., 2015).

On the other hand, Libya has low public debt (6.5% of GDP in 2014) and significant foreign reserves (about USD 109 billion in June 2014 [AfDB/OECD/UNDP, 2015]), although the latter are depleting rapidly as they are needed to finance the current account deficits. Foreign reserves were depleted by USD 3 billion (LYD 3.8 billion) in 2013 and USD 22 billion (LYD 27.5 billion) in 2014.[5] Further depletions in 2015 will have reduced the foreign reserve funds to USD 55 billion (Ianchovichina et al., 2015). The immediate challenge for Libya is to manage its fiscal position, while in the longer term it will be to reduce its dependence on hydrocarbon revenues and vulnerability to external shocks.

The stability of the macroeconomic environment is dependent on the normalisation of the political situation in Libya. The resumption of oil production when the security and political situation improve will fuel government revenues and growth and will facilitate more enabling conditions for private sector and SME development.

3.3. Quality of infrastructure

Roads, seaports, airports, electricity supply and telecommunications networks matter for private sector development. Solid and reliable infrastructure facilitates utilities servicing industrial and production facilities, the efficient flow of goods and services to markets and the rapid flow of information, all of which diminish transaction and trade costs, stimulate economic activity and improve competitiveness. Due to decades of isolation and neglect, Libya's infrastructure was in a poor state even before the 2011 revolution. It has markedly deteriorated since 2010. That year Libya ranked 115 of 139 countries on the "quality of overall infrastructure" indicator of the Global Competitiveness Index (GCI), but by 2014 it had dropped to 144 (Table 3.4).[6] The quality of electricity supply and road infrastructure particularly deteriorated. Much of Libyan infrastructure has been extremely damaged since 2011.

Table 3.4. **Quality of Libya's infrastructure**

	GCI 2014-15		GCI 2013-14		GCI 2010-11	
Indicators for Infrastructure pillar	**Value**	**Rank/144**	**Value**	**Rank/148**	**Value**	**Rank/139**
Quality of overall infrastructure (transport, telephony, energy)	1.9	144	2.3	144	3.2	115
Transport infrastructure						
Quality of roads (out of 7)	2.1	142	2.5	134	3.1	97
Quality of port infrastructure (out of 7)	2.6	131	3.0	124	3.2	116
Quality of air transport infrastructure (out of 7)	2.4	139	2.9	136	2.9	133
Electricity and telephony infrastructure						
Mobile phone subscriptions/100 population	165.0	9	148.2	22	77.9	90
Fixed telephone lines/100 population	12.7	82	12.6	85	17.1	74
Quality of electricity supply (reliability) (out of 7)	2.8	116	3.9	96	4.3	81

Sources: The Global Competitiveness Report (Schwab, 2010, 2013, 2014).

Given its strategic location bordering the Mediterranean and road systems connecting to Tunisia to the west and Egypt to the east, Libya aims to serve as a transit hub. However, the quality of Libyan roads has deteriorated in the past five years along with the security situation in the country. Roads, airports and ports have all been subject to intense fighting and substantial damages, and the use of air transportation has worsened for both firms and individuals since 2011. SMEs surveyed in 2014 reported disruptions along their supply chains due to the closure of seaports or airports, which affected their access to imported goods, petrol and raw materials and their ability to export their products (Calice et al., 2015). This has led to a significant decline in both production levels and revenue. In 2012, Libyan officials estimated at least USD 40 billion would be needed to be spent on transport infrastructure.

In 2011, 44% of Libyan firms – SMEs in particular – considered the unreliability of electric power supply a major constraint to growth. Over 80%, reported suffering from recurrent power outages resulting in productivity losses (World Bank, 2011). The situation worsened after the 2011 events as electric power production dropped. Since then, Libya's electricity grid has significantly deteriorated with shortages in power production and supply. Businesses are also hampered by the time it takes to get connected to the electricity grid. Obtaining the necessary permits and clearances takes 118 days to complete the process, compared to 39 days in Tunisia and 64 days in Egypt (World Bank, 2016c).

A well-developed telecommunications system can contribute to firm productivity. The use of telecommunications reduces transaction costs, increases efficiency in business operations, expands the size and scope of markets and thus can boost private sector development. Libya has deep penetration of mobile subscriptions, and major investments in telecommunications infrastructure were made during the last decades. But more than

USD 1 billion worth of telecom infrastructure has been destroyed since 2011, including about 20% of the country's cellular sites. In addition, internet user penetration rates in Libya are low. In 2014, there were only 17.7 internet users per 100 inhabitants compared to 31.7 per 100 in Egypt and 46.2 per 100 in Tunisia.[7] Internet users also suffer from frequent and extended network interruptions, which among other things can impede business transactions.

The Libyan telecommunications sector is dominated by two state-controlled operators (Al Madar and Libyana). There are plans to privatise one of the operators, creating the first private mobile network in the country. The government drafted the new Telecommunications Bill 2014 and had started the process of establishing an independent regulatory authority. Opening up the telecommunications network to private providers can increase competition, potentially reducing costs and improving service quality. Liberalisation of the telecommunications sector, opening mobile and internet markets to competition and establishing independent regulation can help to sustain and accelerate private sector-led economic growth (World Bank, 2015b).

3.4. Labour market

The labour market in Libya is heavily influenced by the legacy of public sector employment under the state-led redistributive model. The 2011 events and aftermath heightened the many challenges faced by the Libyan labour market. These include overemployment in the bloated public sector, high unemployment – especially among youth and women – low job creation, weak social protection and a lack of social dialogue. Libya's resource curse further distorts the labour market and prevents it from functioning properly.

Addressing the structural labour market inefficiencies, diversifying the economy and empowering a larger and stronger private sector are key to resolving the employment challenges Libya faces. Additional effort will be required to retool the educational system – especially vocational education and training – to prepare a labour force with the appropriate skills needed to develop new sectors identified as priorities for economic diversification.

High unemployment

The labour force participation rate in 2012 was 47.8% (Table 3.5), more or less in line with the average for MENA countries but lower than in other regions of the world (World Bank, 2015c). This indicates a relatively low utilisation of the productive capacity of the Libyan working-age population. The male participation rate (61.0%) is almost twice as high as the female rate (33.8%). At only 38.7%, the employment-to-population ratio is lower than the average in OECD and comparable to other MENA countries and it is higher among

Table 3.5. **Labour market overview, 2012**

	Labour force participation rate (%)			Employment to population ratio (%)			Unemployment rate (%)		
Age group	*Male*	*Female*	*Total*	*Male*	*Female*	*Total*	*Male*	*Female*	*Total*
15-24	24.0	10.7	17.7	14.2	3.4	9.1	40.8	67.8	48.7
25-54	86.2	49.6	67.9	74.4	39.1	56.8	13.7	21.1	16.4
55-64	59.1	9.1	34.9	58.3	8.0	33.9	1.4	12.3	2.9
65+	5.9	0.4	3.4	5.8	0.2	3.5	2.4	50.0	4.5
Total	61.0	33.8	47.8	51.3	25.3	38.7	15.9	25.1	19.0

Source: ILOSTAT Database, International Labour Organization.

Libyan males (51.3%) than females (25.3%).[8] The reported unemployment rate is 19.0%. It is 25.1% for women and 48.7% for young people aged 15-24.[9] Unemployment plays a major role in social discontent, so tackling unemployment, and especially youth unemployment, is a key priority for the Libyan authorities.

Pressure to create job opportunities for young people will continue for some time into the future because 44% of the population is under 25 years of age (26% under 15). A job-creating private sector and economic diversification will be needed to absorb the influx of new labour force entrants and improve labour market indicators. Currently, the private sector is not large or strong enough to play the job creation role required, and the oil sector, although a major contributor to GDP, is not a major employer, accounting for only 2% of employment (43 000 workers) (IMF, 2013).

On the other hand, foreign workers are an important source of labour in Libya as many firms are unable to find qualified Libyans for jobs (Elgazzar et al., 2015). This is the case for both highly skilled jobs in the oil sector (e.g. managers, engineers, high technology professionals) and for low skilled labourers for construction and manual jobs. Prior to 2011, foreign labour was estimated to account for half of the total combined labour force of Libyan nationals and foreigners (Elgazzar et al., 2015). More than 760 000 foreign nationals left Libya during the crisis for security reasons (ETF, 2014). Elgazzar et al. (2015), however, report that in 2012 1.2 million foreign workers were employed in Libya: 430 000 in the formal sector and 800 000 in informal employment.[10] Libyan laws set maximum quotas for the hiring of immigrant workers and restrict them to positions that cannot be filled by Libyan nationals, but there are many abuses. The informal hiring of migrant workers is common, even by large employers and foreign companies. In fact, foreign workers make up the predominant share of all informal workers.

Dependency on public sector jobs

The Libyan labour market is strongly dependent on public sector employment, which causes distortions and contributes to a suboptimal use of labour. Under government nationalisation policies, public sector employment became the primary engine for job creation.[11] As a result, the general government sector and SOEs employ around 84.0% of the workforce;[12] 97.0% of working females and 79.0% of working males (ETF, 2014). Only 2.5% of working women are employed in private sector wage jobs, compared to 11.0% of working men (ETF, 2014). Because of its generous benefits and job security, public sector jobs are the preferred form of employment for Libyans. Private sector employers, including SMEs, have difficulty competing with the public sector for qualified and willing Libyans and are often forced to recruit foreign workers.

The public sector is under pressure to reduce its overemployment and become more efficient, so is not likely to continue to be the job generator of the past. No major reform of the public sector is expected before the resumption of a functioning government. As the number of public sector employment opportunities declines, the expectation is that workers will be absorbed by the private sector, which is unlikely unless it significantly expands. At the same time, public sector workers will need retraining to develop the skills required by private sector employers or to start their own businesses.

Quality of education and workforce skills

The lack of a qualified and appropriately skilled workforce is one of the most important obstacles to economic development and prosperity in Libya. An educated and skilled labour force is critical for developing the private sector, entrepreneurship and SMEs. Higher educational attainment and improved skills of the workforce is essential to diversifying the economy away from oil, moving into more skill-intensive fields and services with high-technology content and improving the overall productivity of private sector enterprises.

The level of educational attainment in Libya has improved significantly in the last decades, with a substantial decrease in the percentage of citizens with no schooling and an increase in the average years of schooling (Table 3.6). The gross enrolment rates in primary education, secondary education and tertiary education are 114%, 104%, and 61% respectively, and almost half of the population aged 25 and older has at least some secondary education (UNDP, 2015).

Table 3.6. **Education attainment of population aged 15+, Libya, 1990-2015**

		Highest education level attained						
		Primary		Secondary		Tertiary		Average years of schooling
	No schooling	Total	Completed	Total	Completed	Total	Completed	
Year	percentage of population aged 15 and over							
1990	36.9	29.8	18.2	30.2	15.9	3.1	1.6	5.1
1995	30.4	29.2	20.3	36.3	19.1	4.1	2.0	5.9
2000	24.9	28.6	21.9	36.3	19.1	10.1	5.0	6.9
2005	21.1	28.0	22.7	34.6	18.6	16.3	8.4	7.6
2010	18.0	27.7	23.4	32.6	17.8	21.8	11.7	8.3
2015	16.3	24.2	21.3	29.0	15.8	30.5	16.2	9.1

Sources: Barro and Lee (2013) for 1990-2010 data. 2015 data from the Barrolee dataset "Education Attainment for Total Population 2015-2040", http://barrolee.com/data/oup_download_c.htm/.

Education is compulsory from 6 to 15 and free through to university and post-graduate education. Efforts to expand higher education opportunities across the country have been successful, with colleges and universities located in all 12 big cities, although these are often overcrowded. Schools at each level are directing more Libyan students into science and technology in an effort to prepare graduates to meet future workforce requirements.

While the level of education of Libyans compares relatively well to other developing countries, the quality of educational programmes leaves many individuals unprepared for the labour market. Libya performs poorly in the GCI 2014-15 on the overall quality of the educational system, ranking 128 out of 144 countries on "quality of basic education" and 144 on "quality of the higher education system" (Schwab, 2014). There is a mismatch between the skills acquired through the education system and the competencies needed by the labour market (Braun, 2011). Limited, if any, consultation takes place between vocational education and training institutions and the private sector to identify the skills needed by employers. Consequently, training programmes do not always match employers' needs. As a result, individuals who enrol in vocational education and training do not necessarily have greater chances to be employed. Libyan firms consider "an inadequately educated workforce" as one of the top three most problematic factors for doing business (Schwab, 2014).

There have been attempts to improve the educational system. For example, the Libyan Board for Technical and Vocational Education (NBTVE) planned to establish a vocational education and training system across the more than 100 higher education colleges and technical institutes (Clark, 2013).Other initiatives have attempted to increase co-operation with the private sector and improve higher education.

Deficiencies in labour institutions

The Ministry of Labour and Manpower is responsible for regulation of the labour market in Libya, ensuring employers are in compliance with labour legislation and overseeing a network of 72 job centres across the country. The job centres are tasked with job matching and placement services, designed to positively impact the labour market and individuals' prospects for finding work, particularly in the private sector. However, the centres were not performing since they lacked clear direction, were poorly organised and staffed with underqualified and poorly trained personnel. They also focused on meeting employment needs of the public sector, with minimal linkages with the private sector (Upper Quartile, 2013). A strategy is needed to modernise and upgrade the employment service, ensure staff training capacity is available and that a management structure is in place to support the new method of working.

The job centres could be instrumental in offering supplementary worker training and subsidising human resource development for SMEs. Promoting the services of job centres among businesses, setting up an online system for job matching, and engaging local SMEs in the design of active labour market policies would be first steps in the right direction (Upper Quartile, 2013). Job centres could align their training offer to the needs of employers, such as in Information Technology (IT) skills, systems certification and English-language proficiency. They could also offer support for entrepreneurship training to encourage unemployed Libyans to start their own businesses. Such programmes exist in many countries, typically providing employment benefits for the registered unemployed who are interested in starting their own business, have a viable business idea, and are willing to undertake an intensive period of self-employment training to gain basic entrepreneurial skills, develop a business plan and learn business management essentials.

By 2012, there was no labour market information system (KDS/KOREATECH, 2013). Although the ministry has developed several databases, they do not seem to be comprehensive or accurate (World Bank, 2015a). Without accurate, reliable and up-to-date data, there is no concrete evidence to ground labour market analysis or sound policy making for either Libyan nationals or foreign workers. The ETF (2014) urges the Ministry of Labour and Manpower and the Statistics Bureau to work together to address labour market information gaps, develop appropriate information tools and improve their labour market analysis capacity.

Reforms to the unemployment reporting system are also required. It is a common practice for individuals who are not working in the public sector to register as unemployed simply because they do not have public employment. Under the current system, even individuals working in the public sector but seeking promotion, or those working on a formal contract in the private sector, can go to the Labour Office and register as unemployed if they wish as there is no national database or IT system to verify their situation (ETF, 2014). A comprehensive e-government project for a "national identification number system" was introduced in 2014; its implementation would contribute to more accurate statistics.

The World Bank advocates for the development of a comprehensive jobs strategy that will implement labour market reforms and interventions (Elgazzar et al., 2015). Skills and self-employment training programmes for nationals should be one of the priorities, with the aim of reducing the gap between skills supply and demand, as well as implementation of school-to-work transition programmes involving the private sector, in-company vocational training, job coaching programmes and job seeking services (ETF, 2014).

Labour regulations

Labour policies and institutions, including regulations, collective representation, active labour market programmes and social security schemes, can in principle address labour market failures that can lead to excessive turnover, unsafe workplaces and underinvestment in training (World Bank, 2012). However, overly restrictive labour laws and regulations may discourage employers from hiring, thus reducing employment, or promote the hiring of informal workers, who are not covered by official employment contracts or by social security benefits. Hiring and termination restrictions can slow down labour reallocation and prevent firms from making labour force decisions that will lead to increased productivity. On the other hand, if labour regulations and rules are too loose, or not enforced, issues such as poor information, unequal bargaining power or inadequate risk management will not be addressed (World Bank, 2012).

Labour Law No. 12/2010 replaced the outdated Labour Law of 1958. It regulates forms of contracting and the rights and duties of employees and employers. It also determines the relations and procedures among the employer, employee and employment agencies for foreign and national employees alike, specifies dispute-settling mechanisms and types of competent courts and introduces equality between male and female workers. The law requires all employers to notify the employment office of the name, address, activity and number of workers at the beginning of a project. All necessary procedures are to be taken to protect the safety and health of their workers, and, through labour contracts, employers are to inform workers of the internal regulations regarding working hours, penalties, holidays, participation in the social security fund and type of insurance offered. The government also seeks to further reform the labour law to conform to international labour standards regarding eight-hour work days, labour wages vacations and end-of-service benefits.

An improvement in the new law is that it applies the same rules and standards to workers in the public and private sectors. The previous labour law applied to only the private sector, while public sector workers were subject to the Civil Service Law, which offered more job security guarantees, generous non-wage benefits, allowances and subsidies, and sharp restrictions on dismissal. This caused labour market distortions in favour of public sector employment. The new law also provides for equal treatment of foreign workers and Libyan nationals with respect to rights, duties, courts and procedures. If effectively implemented, these improvements could address labour market distortions by creating a more level playing field for employers and workers, irrespective of their working environment or nationality.

The new labour law still lacks clarity regarding the hiring of Libyan versus foreign workers. In alignment with Investment Law No. 9/2010, it applies a quota system requiring all national and foreign employers to hire a minimum percentage of Libyan nationals and incur the cost of their training. But these laws differ in the proportion of Libyan nationals to be employed in a foreign project. The new labour law requires a minimum of 75%, while the 2010 investment law only requires 30%. This point needs to be addressed to avoid problems during implementation of investment projects or in the settling of disputes, considering also migrant labour as a mechanism to find the skills needed that match the job requirements. The national quota system in some cases leaves companies with only the options of hiring and paying domestic workers who do not contribute to the company's productivity or investing a considerable amount of resources on extensive training and mentoring. As well, migrant workers do not routinely receive labour contracts and hence do not enjoy the same rights as Libyan nationals, an issue that will have to be carefully monitored under the terms of the labour law.

The impact of the new labour law on smaller employers remains to be seen, especially in terms of the appropriate level of flexibility for hiring and dismissal in employment contracts and the requirements for social charges. Most firms surveyed in the World Bank study of labour market dynamics supported reforming labour policy with respect to social protection, contracts and foreign labour, although only 56% of the companies were familiar with the new labour code (Elgazzar et al., 2015), which flags an information failure. Of those familiar, 15% advocated for reforms that would facilitate the hiring of foreign workers to fill the need for highly-skilled workers, although most firms were unclear about the actual labour regulations. Six percent advocated for easier contracting procedures – reduced complexity and administrative costs – and promoted an improvement in employers' rights, particularly related to greater flexibility in the dismissal of under-performing Libyan national workers.

3.5. Financial markets and access to finance

Well-functioning financial markets are essential for channelling an adequate supply of finance to private sector firms, including SMEs and start-ups. This normally involves a mix of deposit-taking banks, insurance companies, pension funds, investment banks, microfinance institutions, trade credit and leasing companies, venture capital funds and business angels, offering a mix of diverse financial products (e.g. loan products, factoring and equity instruments) adapted to projects at different stages of business development. There are three main requirements for well-functioning financial markets. First, lenders and investors on the supply side should have adequate finance and capacities to assess the risks and returns of investment in SMEs and entrepreneurs. Second, entrepreneurs and SME managers on the demand side should have the skills, knowledge and financial literacy to locate the most appropriate available sources of finance and act as competent stewards of investments. Third, there should be a transparent infrastructure for financial intermediation to minimise information asymmetries among parties, and it should be embedded within a regulatory and legal framework that protects the legal rights of all market participants. These requirements are missing in Libya.

Low level of credit to the private sector

The financial sector in Libya is small and underdeveloped. Compared with high-income OECD countries, and even MENA countries, the volume of domestic credit to the private sector and the volume of credit provided by the banking sector represent a small share of Libya's GDP. This indicator is one of the main variables in assessing the level of financial development of a country – the higher the measure, the higher the level of financial resources or financing to the private sector in a country.[13] In 2014, domestic credit to the private sector in Libya was only 27.0% of GDP, up from 9.3% in 2010, but still very low compared to the average of 37.0% of GDP in the developing MENA countries and 150.0% of GDP in high-income OECD countries (Figure 3.7).

Bank lending is an important source of funding to the private sector, typically representing the largest sector in the financial system. The level of domestic credit to the private sector by banks is a measure of banking sector depth and financial sector development in terms of size. A low percentage of private sector credit by banks as a share of GDP indicates financing obstacles for businesses, which could also be a reflection of tight regulations. Libya's performance on this indicator improved from 2010 to 2014 but falls far below that of the average for developing MENA countries, particularly Morocco and Tunisia (Figure 3.8). This demonstrates low financial intermediation of the banking sector.

Figure 3.7. **Domestic credit to the private sector (% of GDP), 2010 and 2014**

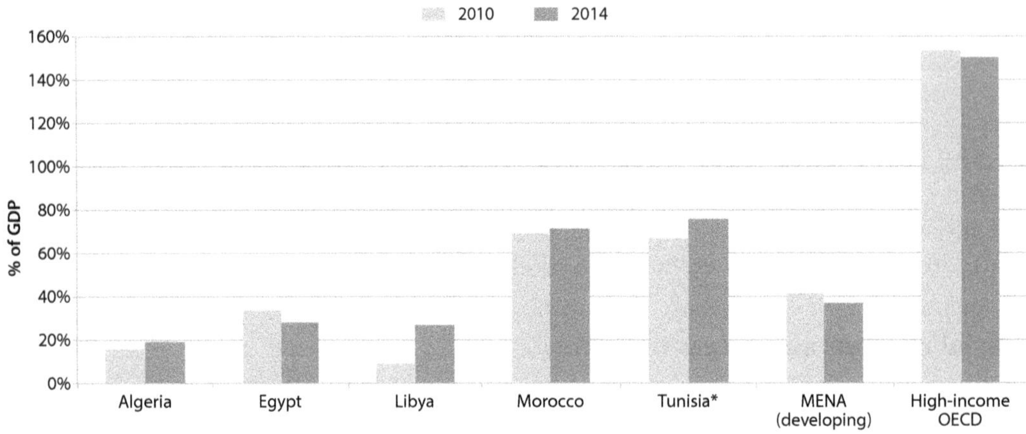

Note: "Domestic credit to private sector" refers to financial resources provided to the private sector by financial corporations (monetary authorities and deposit money banks, as well as other financial corporations who have data available, such as finance and leasing companies, money lenders, insurance corporations, pension funds and foreign exchange companies) through loans, purchases of non-equity securities, trade credit and other accounts receivable that establish a claim for repayment (http://data.worldbank.org/indicator/FS.AST.PRVT.GD.ZS).

* Tunisia data is 2013, not 2014.

Source: World Development Indicators Database, World Bank, October 2015 edition, http://data.worldbank.org/products/wdi/.

Figure 3.8. **Domestic credit to the private sector by banks, 2010 and 2014**

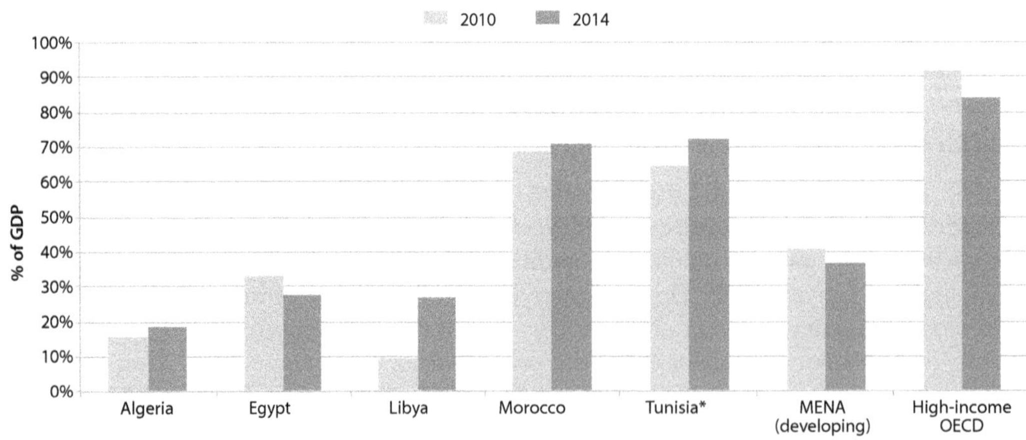

Note: "Domestic credit to private sector by banks" refers to financial resources provided to the private sector by deposit-taking corporations (except central banks), through loans, purchases of non-equity securities, trade credits and other accounts receivable that establish a claim for repayment. For some countries these claims include credit to public enterprises (World Development Indicators).

* Tunisia data is 2013, not 2014.

Source: World Development Indicators Database, World Bank, October 2015 edition, http://data.worldbank.org/products/wdi.

Libya is the worst performer globally on financial market development according to the GCI 2014-15 (Schwab, 2014).[14] Performance is weak on all indicators. This includes the availability and affordability of financial services, ease of access to loans, financing through the local equity market, venture capital availability, soundness of banks, regulation of securities exchanges and legal rights index.

Libya has 15 commercial banks, which account for 81% of the total assets in the financial sector (Troug and Sbia, 2015). Five are state-owned, accounting for 90% of the deposit base, eight are private banks and two banks are owned jointly by the Libyan government and foreign states. Public sector banks control more than 85% of banking sector assets (Crisp, 2013), in spite of efforts to liberalise and transform the banking sector in 2005 with the Libyan Bank Law (No. 1/2005) and the partial privatisations that took place in 2007.

Even though state-owned banks are heavily capitalised, the extent and diversity of financial services is very limited (Dempsey, 2013). Non-performing loans are at high levels,[15] and supervision of the banking sector is weak with potential for corruption and favouritism in the loan-granting process. Weak property rights prevent borrowers from meeting collateral requirements, and credit information systems are extremely nascent, making it almost impossible for banks to assess the credit risk of borrowers. Moreover, banking sector skills are very weak at all levels of the financial sector (World Bank, 2013). The Central Bank of Libya has been taking actions to modernise the banking system and introduce new standards of accounting and training, but efforts have been impeded due to the political instability and ongoing conflict.

Adoption of Islamic Banking

An Islamic banking law was enacted in 2013 (Islamic Bank Law No. 1/2013) banning the use of interest in all civil and commercial transactions (i.e. the charging or paying of interest on deposits and loans) and requiring financial institutions to comply with Islamic Sharia law. It should have entered into force on 1 January 2015, but it has been delayed because of the instability in the country. The government's decision to implement a strict Islamic banking regime has created uncertainty within the financial sector (World Bank, 2013). In the meantime, financial institutions have been scrambling to find Sharia-compliant financing mechanisms. To mitigate the shock to Libya's financial system of the transition to Islamic finance and to facilitate its smooth introduction, the World Bank recommends that Libya adopt a dual "Islamic-Conventional" banking system, which was successfully adopted in other countries, including Qatar, Oman and the United Arab Emirates (World Bank, 2013).

Law No. 1/2013 provides for the creation of a Goodwill Lending Fund to make interest free loans (*Qard Hassan*), to be set up under supervision of the Central Bank of Libya. This offers a substitute for commercial lending transactions, but the operational details of such a fund are still unclear.

The move to Islamic banking may be favourable to Libyan SMEs, as one of the major reasons for not approaching banks for loans is their aversion to interest-based financing (Wahab and Abdesamed, 2012). On the other hand, Islamic banking may create a hindrance to foreign investors, who are comfortable with traditional forms of bank financing. Some financial institutions may consider using offshore structures that fall outside of the Libyan law, especially concerning the financing of foreign interests in Libya.

Underdeveloped equity markets

Apart from on an informal basis through family and friends, the equity market in Libya is underdeveloped. The absence of a venture capital industry limits opportunities for SMEs with growth potential and innovative start-ups to access risk financing for their ventures. The government introduced a law in 2007 for the creation of the Libyan stock market primarily to support the privatisation of SOEs, but it is not well-capitalised, has few listings and does not have a high volume of trading.

3.6. Investment policy and legal framework

The presence of a transparent and predictable regulatory framework is a critical determinant of a country's Foreign Direct Investment (FDI) attractiveness. The degree of openness to foreign investment, the protection of investors' property rights and mechanisms for settling investment disputes are core investment policy issues that underpin efforts to create a quality investment environment (OECD, 2015b). Uncertainty about the enforceability of legal rights and obligations raises the cost of capital and reduces attractiveness for foreign investors.

FDI is critical to rebuilding the Libyan economy and strengthening the private sector, including SMEs. Apart from capital, FDI plays a strong role in bringing in much needed new technology, management techniques, technical expertise and connections to global markets. However, Libya performs poorly on FDI attraction compared with other countries, ranking 97 out of 111 countries (index value of 28/100) on the Global Foreign Direct Investment Country Attractiveness Index (GFICA) and 15 out of 18 Arab countries.[16] There is also a significant gap between its FDI potential and actual performance compared to other transition countries (Efhialelbum and Flatau, 2013), especially in the non-hydrocarbon sectors.

Libya's efforts to attract FDI are relatively recent. Until the 1990s, FDI was only permitted in the oil sector through sovereign contracts to which the state was a party. A major reform to attract FDI was the enactment of the Encouragement of Foreign Capital Investment Law No. 5/1997, later amended by the Promotion of Investment of Foreign Capital Law No. 7/2003. These laws allowed 100% foreign ownership of licensed companies in a broad range of sectors, including industry, health, tourism, services and agriculture. Decree No. 171/2006 made it much easier for foreign investors to do business in Libya, allowing them to form joint venture companies with Libyan shareholders with a minimum capital of LYD 1 million and retain 65% of the shareholdings.

Although joint ventures are highly regulated and the number of local partners may be limited, many foreign investors choose to enter joint venture or joint stock companies with Libyan resident companies because it can present certain advantages, for example, when bidding for government contracts. As a result, Libya saw significant growth in the volume of FDI inflows from 2004, mounting to almost 7% of GDP in 2007 (Figure 3.9). From 2003 to 2010, over 350 investment projects were approved, creating jobs for over 50 000 Libyans and 15 000 foreigners, with projects in diverse activities, including tourism, health and education (Alfituri, 2013).[17] However, since 2007, FDI flows have been constantly decreasing, grinding almost to a halt in 2014.

The Encouragement of both National and Foreign Investment Law No. 9/2010 (known as the investment law) replaced the previous foreign investment laws. This new law lifted many FDI restrictions and provides a series of incentives, such as tax and customs exemptions on equipment, a five-year income tax exemption, a tax exemption on re-invested profits and exemptions on production tax and export fees for goods produced for export markets. It also allows foreign investors to transfer net profits overseas, defer losses to future years, import necessary goods and hire foreign labour if local labour is unavailable. Foreign workers can acquire residency permits and entry/re-entry visas, renewable for five years, and transfer earnings overseas.

Figure 3.9. **Libya's trends in net FDI inflows and share of GDP, 2000-14**

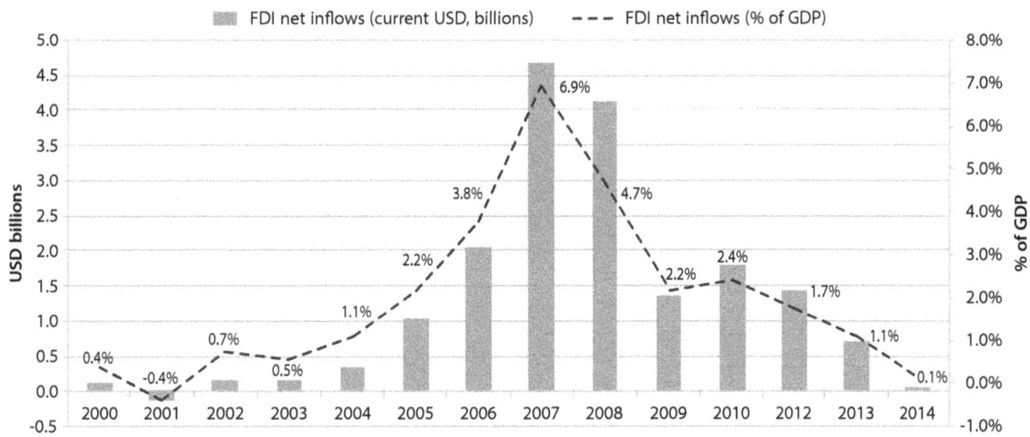

Note: No available data for 2011.

Source: World Development Indicators database, 29 December 2015 edition, World Bank.

The law regulates the establishment of foreign-owned companies – which can be fully owned if the foreign investment exceeds LYD 5 million – and setting up of branches and representative offices. Branches are allowed to be opened in a large number of sectors. This includes construction for contracts over LYD 50 million; electricity works; oil exploration, drilling and installation projects; telecommunications construction and installation; industry; surveying and planning; installation and maintenance of medical machines and equipment; and hospital management. However, the investment law restricts full ownership of investment projects, except in the case of limited liability companies, and requires 30% of workers to be Libyan nationals and receive training. Foreign investors are still prevented from owning land and property in Libya and are allowed only the temporary use of real estate.

One of the most significant benefits included in the new investment law is the provision of legislative protection against nationalisation and expropriation unless accompanied by a law or judicial ruling. Nevertheless, the law does not outline specific procedures to be followed in disputes between the state and the investor and leaves some decisions and rulings regarding the extension, suspension or halting of foreign projects to the discretion of the minister of economy.

Despite these attempts to create opportunities for foreign investment, the impact of the investment law has not yet been felt. There was little time for FDI to recover from the effects of the 2008-09 global financial crises before the advent of the 2011 revolution. Since then, the unstable environment in Libya has not been conducive to foreign investment. Fragile economies riven by conflict face additional difficulties in attracting private investment due to high political and economic instability and an environment not conducive to commerce (World Bank, 2014b). Reconstruction needs, severely underserved consumer demand and available natural resources present Libya with many opportunities for domestic and foreign investors. In a post-conflict scenario, infrastructure investment projects, facilitated through public-private partnerships (PPPs), could play a key role in accelerating structural transition and speeding up job creation. They could also provide a foundation for sustainable growth and integration in the global economy over the longer term.

Several restrictions on foreign investors were introduced in 2012 and 2013, which are likely to have a negative impact on future FDI.[18] The decision to limit the foreign share of Libyan companies to 49% is a major disincentive to foreign investors who may seek more attractive majority-ownership investment opportunities in other countries. While it may be reasonable to set some limitations on the entry of foreign companies in order to protect the fledgling Libyan private sector, it is also important to attract foreign capital and expertise and encourage international businesses to work alongside Libyan businesspeople, create jobs for Libyan nationals and invest in training and development. The constant changes to laws and regulations affecting foreign investment since 2011 add to the uncertainty regarding investment decisions.

Due to ongoing conflict and a lack of an effective government since 2011, the legislative and judicial institutions have not been able to apply the investment laws or test their efficacy in practice. The PIB is the most important investment promotion institution in Libya, established in 2009 to assume responsibility for the Libyan privatisation programme and oversee and regulate FDI activities in the industrial sector under the investment law. However, the PIB has focused on privatisation efforts, and it has not sufficiently fulfilled its role as an investment promotion agency (G8/UK Presidency Deauville Partnership, 2013).

The PIB did, however, introduce the single window system for investors in 2013, offering a range of services, such as issuing licenses, processing customs duty and tax exemptions, commercial registration, approving project supplies and supervising labour contracts, including worker visas and residency permits. The PIB's investment promotion role should be strengthened. Stronger co-ordination between the PIB, the Libyan Investment Authority[19] and enterprise development agencies could help facilitate joint ventures and direct investment in existing private enterprises.

Most countries in the region have lifted restrictive capital requirements. In Algeria, where the 49-51 investment rule still applies, there is a desire to amend it with a view to attract FDI. In developing a solid policy framework for investment, the government of Libya could look at Iraq's experience of working actively to improve its framework to attract investors despite the high levels of risk in the country (Box 3.1).

Foreign investors can also set up operations in one of Libya's offshore free zones, established under Law No. 9/2000 on Free Zones and Transit Trade. These zones aim to foster the development of manufacturing facilities and exports, create employment and training opportunities for Libyans, transfer technology and knowledge, and diversify the economy. Investors in free zone activities benefit from expedited business establishment processes, free repatriation of capital and profits, energy supply at local rates, exemption from commercial registration, tax, custom duty restrictions, exchange controls and monitoring, and vast areas of land on lease for up to 30 years (renewable).

Box 3.1. Iraq's investment policy framework

In 2007, the government of Iraq requested OECD support for improving policies and institutions to attract private investment into the country. In response, the MENA-OECD Investment Programme launched the Iraq Project, which helps identify and support policy reforms through research and policy dialogue.

Iraq's current political and security situation are critical barriers to attracting greater amounts of investment. However, large gaps in the investment policy framework and institutional capacity also existed.

While Iraq's 2006 investment law fosters investment, the complementary legislation and the way the law is implemented do not protect investors. For example, investors cannot easily access land for investment projects. In addition, investment promotion and facilitation capacities are low.

The Iraq Project has achieved the following since 2013:

- It has helped the government develop a more attractive investment policy framework for investment by analysing and developing recommendations for the second amendment to the 2006 investment law. The amendment was enacted in October 2015 with some of the OECD recommendations.
- It has actively supported other legal initiatives to integrate Iraq into international investment policy frameworks. It aided the government in joining the Washington Convention on Investor-State Dispute Settlement in November 2015 and advised on a new draft of an international arbitration law. Workshops on bilateral investment treaties have also been conducted as part of the project.
- More than 60 staff members from the national and provincial investment promotion agencies have been trained on developing investment marketing material, handling investor inquiries and presenting materials to investors. Moreover, the project has worked on developing investment files to formulate and market investment opportunities in Iraq.

Source: Middle East and Africa Division, Global Relations Secretariat, OECD.

3.7. Trade policies

Trade policies influence the size of markets for the output of firms and can shape both foreign and domestic investment (OECD, 2015b). Due to decades of economic isolation, trade sanctions in the 1980s and restrictive trade policies until the end of the 1990s, the volume of Libyan non-oil exports did not increase much over the years. Since 2000, trade liberalisation policies were adopted by the government including price liberalisation, setting exchange rates and law no. 11/2010 regulating the securities market. In 2005, the state removed customs tariffs, simplified customs procedures, rescinded Decree no. 12/2005 that restricted the importation of certain goods to a sole agent and further reduced the number of prohibited items from 31 to 17. It also reduced customs taxes – limiting them only to consumption tax – exempted all goods from import license rules and allowed SMEs to import necessary production material with greater flexibility. These legislative changes had a positive effect on encouraging investors, especially SMEs, towards imports, as did the reduction of restrictions on commercial banking transactions and a simplified process of issuing letters of credit.

The adoption of trade liberalisation policies has resulted in an upsurge in the Libyan export and import index during the past few years, leading to a positive trade balance. This trend has, however, been disrupted by the events since 2011 (Figure 3.10). In 2012, exports rebounded to USD 61 billion, although since then they have declined. Libyan demand for imports has also been rising, reaching USD 32.5 billion in 2012. Machines, semi-processed products, foodstuffs, transportation equipment and consumption goods constituted the bulk of imports, with approximately half of Libya's food needs being supplied through imports.

Figure 3.10. **Trends in Libya's exports and imports, 2000-14**

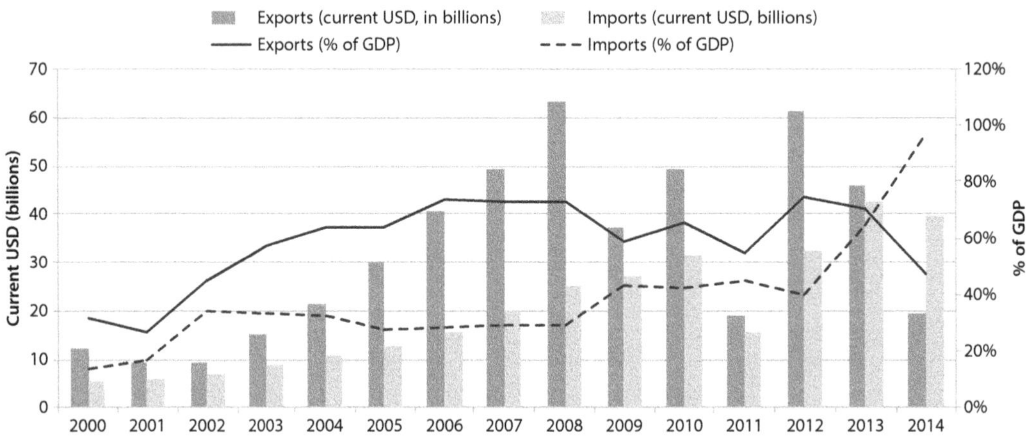

Source: World Development Indicators database, December 2015 edition, World Bank.

Trade liberalisation policies mainly boosted the oil sector.[20] If oil exports are excluded, Libya would have a negative trade balance, so it is important in the future to increase exports in the non-oil sectors. SMEs have not been effectively targeted to benefit from trade liberalisation. In the initial stages, SMEs may depend on local markets, but with the appropriate capacity building and incentives they can be encouraged to develop export markets in subsequent stages. By doing so, SMEs can contribute to the diversification of the economy and help transform Libya into a state that does not depend exclusively on its oil exports. At the same time, Libya needs to identify potential products for export markets to diminish its dependence on oil exports.

Libya is underdeveloped in terms of trade in services, which should not be ignored in its trade liberalisation efforts, as increasing sophistication in services exports is associated with higher economic growth (Mishra et al., 2011). From 2008-13 trade in services averaged 10.4% of GDP, well below the average for the developing MENA region of about 19.0%.[21] The largest services exports in the Libyan economy are transport, insurance, communication and travel services. In 2010, transport and travel services accounted for more than 78.0% of services exports.[22] Trade in all of the services sectors was dramatically affected in 2011. Nevertheless, in a post-conflict scenario transportation services will present significant growth potential, particularly in the area of transit trade (OECD, 2014).

Libya's trade relations are hindered by its limited number of bilateral country agreements and membership in regional economic blocs, largely comprising neighbouring countries, such as the Council of Arab Economic Unity (CAEU), the Greater Arab Free Trade Area (GAFTA), the Arab Maghreb Union, the Community of Sahel-Saharan States and the Common Market for Eastern and Southern Africa (COMESA). In 2004, Libya became an applicant country to the World Trade Organisation (WTO), but neither did it submit its memorandum on the foreign trade regime nor did it hold any discussions. When the security and political situation in Libya stabilises, there will be an opportunity to build on the 2013 US-Libya Trade Agreement, which will open up opportunities for trade with the United States, and pick up negotiations with the EU on the framework agreement on trade, begun in 2008 but suspended in February 2011. Libya should also reinitiate the WTO accession process.

Libya performs relatively poorly on the World Bank's Logistic Performance Index (LPI)[23] (World Bank, 2014a). The government should take actions to improve trade facilitation, reducing the costs of trade-related transport logistics and increasing the reliability and timeliness of shipments. High transport and transaction costs impose important obstacles in exploiting opportunities presented by world trading systems. And since these costs are often fixed, they weigh disproportionately heavy on smaller firms (Chauffour, 2013). Improving the quality of logistics services – e.g. trucking, warehousing, freight forwarding – and the efficiency of customs clearance processes – e.g. automating import and export procedures, creating a single window for foreign trade and further developing the quality of trade and transport-related infrastructure – could facilitate trade flows and supply chain linkages between producers and international buyers.

Free zone enterprises are another vehicle to promote and facilitate transit trade. Law no. 9/2000 regulates free zone enterprises, requiring paid-up capital of at least USD 100 000. It also warrants special exemptions and benefits similar to those for an investment enterprise (e.g. exemption from customs on machinery, equipment, parts and supplies needed for its operations and from income tax for five years). Free zone enterprises have access to storage facilities for goods to be imported and exported and can carry out repacking, assembly and mixing of goods for re-exporting or sales in the domestic market. A free zone enterprise can also be formed to provide professional services needed by activities in the free zones. However, with only one free zone in Misrata, Libya has not had the same success as Egypt and the Gulf States in attracting free zone enterprises. More free zones outside Tripoli and Benghazi are anticipated and these could be very useful in stimulating trade activity.

3.8. Innovation system

Innovation, in the form of new products, processes, and ways of managing, is essential to economic growth and to realising Libya's diversification objective. The concept of a National Innovation System (NIS) rests on the premise that fostering linkages among the players involved in innovation – primarily private enterprises, universities and public research institutes – is key to improving technology performance (OECD, 1997). In turn, this aids in boosting labour productivity, enhancing competitiveness and increasing welfare. Innovation policy should take a broad and inclusive perspective, supporting modest and incremental innovations, as well as innovations based on high technologies (CMI, 2013). This notion is particularly relevant for the Libyan context where the vast majority of companies do not have a technological base to drive new products or processes. A vibrant Information and Communications Technology (ICT) sector is also crucial to enabling innovation.

Poor performance on indicators of technological readiness and innovation

Libya as a whole performs very poorly on all GCI indicators of technological readiness and innovation, ranking between 140 and 144 of 144 countries on most of them (Schwab, 2014) (Table 3.7). It performs slightly better on the availability of scientists and engineers. Libya has a large pool of overseas engineers and technicians who were educated in the

West. Developing linkages with this diaspora could bring a much needed technical human resource capacity to Libya's aid in spearheading innovative technology enterprises.

Table 3.7. **Strength of Libya's innovation performance and technological readiness**

R&D innovation – indicators	Value	Rank/144
Capacity for innovation	2.5	144
Quality of scientific research institutions	1.7	143
Company spending on R&D	1.8	144
University-industry collaboration in R&D	1.7	144
Government procurement of advanced technology products	1.9	143
Availability of scientists and engineers	3.3	119
International patents, applications/million inhabitants	0.0	124
Intellectual property protection	1.8	143
Venture capital availability*	1.6	142
Technological readiness – indicators	**Value**	**Rank/144**
Technological adoption		
Availability of latest technologies	3.1	140
Firm-level technology absorption	3.2	142
FDI and technology transfer	2.7	144
ICT use		
Individuals using the internet, %	16.5	108
Fixed broadband Internet subscriptions/100 inhabitants	1.0	106
International Internet bandwidth, kilobits (kb) per second	21.5	82

* The venture capital availability indicator was added to the innovation list because of its importance to an effective innovation system.

Source: Schwab (2014), *The Global Competitiveness Report 2014-2015*: 249.

Public expenditure on R&D in Arab countries is less than 1% of GDP (CMI, 2013). Although there is no official data for Libya, the public R&D expenditure to GDP is likely to be less than 0.5%. Private sector engagement in innovation is limited and the innovation performance of enterprises is weak. As long as political uncertainty and security issues prevail, the private sector is unlikely to invest in R&D or innovative activities because of the higher risks and longer-term returns.

Weak protection of intellectual property

Protection of investors' inventions at the national and global levels fosters innovation, boosts consumer confidence in product quality and specifications, helps open new markets to investments in the technology and electronics sectors and encourages foreign investors to increase the volume of investments in host countries where they know their intellectual property rights are safeguarded. To foster innovation in Libya, intellectual property protection needs strengthening. Libya scores 1.8 out of 7.0 and ranks 143 out of 144 countries (Schwab, 2014). It also ranks last among 129 countries on the intellectual property rights indicator in the *2015 International Property Rights Index* (IPRI), far below the other North African countries (Table 3.8) (Property Rights Alliance, 2015).[24] Libya's intellectual property rights (IPR) score declined from a score of 3.3 in 2013 to 2.5 in 2012 and 1.2 in 2015.

Table 3.8. **Performance of Libya on the Intellectual Property Rights Index, 2015**

	Strength of IPR	
Country	Score	Rank/129
Libya	**1.2**	**129**
Algeria	3.4	111
Tunisia	4.2	89
Egypt	4.3	83
Morocco	5.0	62
MENA average (14 countries, including the GCCs)	4.6	N/A
Average for 129 countries	5.1	N/A

Note: Scores are out of 10. Rank is out of 129 countries. Three IPR indicators are covered in the score: *(1)* protection of intellectual property rights; *(2)* patent protection; and *(3)* copyright protection.

Source: Property Rights Alliance (2015), *International Property Rights Index: 2015 Report*, http://internationalpropertyrightsindex.org/.

Libya does not have an intellectual property law. In lieu of, Article 1286 of Commercial Law No. 23/2010 covers a set of rules which seek to protect intellectual innovations and the non-material aspects of industrial and commercial projects. It prohibits infringement of trademarks and transgression on registered trade names and logos, bans all acts of forgery, trademark or logo counterfeiting and all other forms of intellectual property violations, and outlines the nature of financial and criminal procedures against those violations. The law provides for enforcement of the rules regulating registered industrial designs and models as well as information systems. Some additional laws providing protection of IPR have been passed, such as law No. 7 of 1984 and law No. 8 of 1959 on patents, commercial designs and models. However, these laws are outdated and lack up-to-date provisions for protecting IPR in Libya. The Trademark Office in the Ministry of Economy is responsible for enforcing the Law of Consumer and Intellectual Property Protection, but trademark violations are widespread, especially in the retail sector, and enforcement generally requires a specific legal claim.[25]

The IMF has called upon Libya to bring its IPR regime in line with international best practice, although renewed efforts of the Ministry of Economy to deal with the problem are yet to produce evidence of clear progress.[26] IPR protection laws need to be updated as they are a critical factor in encouraging private enterprises and SMEs to pursue innovation activities.

Fragmentation and lack of co-ordination of innovation system components

There is no formal innovation support system in the country and government's efforts to develop components of an NIS have been modest (OECD, 2014). Certain components of an innovation system do exist but lack co-ordination and linkages with private sector enterprises and SMEs are weak. For example, the Industrial Research Center (IRC) at the Ministry of Industry provides professional services with the aim of introducing technology to industrial institutions, developing export capacity, supporting new industrial start-ups and promoting capital investment in local industries, and facilitating procedures for the registration of intellectual property, such as patent applications and fees. The IRC hosts a number of industry laboratories and an office for industrial property rights in Libya. The Libyan Authority for Research, Science and Technology (LARST), under the Ministry of Higher Education and Scientific Research, is responsible for 33 research centres in all scientific fields, which could be tapped into for potential viable projects. Moreover, there are a small number of business incubators, four of which are based on university campuses, which could be a source of innovation projects. However, these existing institutions are not linked to an innovation ecosystem.

There are also a number of gaps in the innovation system, which need to be filled over time. These include venture capital, innovation grant funds, technology transfer offices to focus on the technologies brought in by foreign firms and innovation clusters built around knowledge-based sectors (e.g. green economy, renewable energy and new materials). Increasing funding for innovation support programmes would help develop and sustain innovative entrepreneurial activities.

Libyan scientific research has suffered from a lack of vision, the absence of a national policy and strategy for science and technology, and innovation, a lack of clear objectives and priorities and a weak relationship between the scientific research centres, higher education institutions and the business sector.[27] Knowledge production in the form of patents, scientific publications and articles, technology licensing fees and royalties is very low.

The issue of co-ordination of the innovation policy framework and its delivery is still a potential problem and needs to be addressed. The OECD (2012) highlights the cross-departmental nature of innovation policy, which touches many policy areas. Among these are research, industry, education, trade, finance and competition. Countries that have succeeded in establishing a well-functioning innovation system have established co-ordinating bodies for innovation policy, positioning them at the prime ministerial level, with the capacity to make decisions and the authority to implement them. Such bodies have been decisive in putting innovation policy at the forefront of national development strategies.

A promising development in 2012 was the establishment of a national committee to develop a National Strategy for Science, Technology and Innovation in partnership and collaboration with all economic sectors. The final strategy was submitted to the National Planning Council (NPC) in March 2014, outlining the innovation policy, the framework for an NIS in Libya and actions to stimulate and support innovation, such as innovation prizes and the development of science and technology parks. Some announcements for initiatives were made after the release of the strategy, but progress is likely to be slow under the current context. In early 2014, for example, LARST launched a Technology and Innovation Parks Department with the aim of creating a stimulating environment for innovation and technology transfer and building a knowledge-based economy. This will lead to the creation of technology parks and innovation centres, which would be an important complement to other components of the innovation system.

3.9. SOE policies

The state is deeply involved in utilities, oil and gas, agriculture, construction, real estate development and manufacturing, and the corporate economy is dominated by large state-owned and controlled enterprises. According to a study by the Libya Institute for Advanced Studies, many Libyans consider that the government should not be involved in the production and delivery of products that can be more effectively delivered by the private sector (LIAS, 2014). Making room for private enterprise activity and building the capacity for Libya to become more productive would require government commitment and a programme of privatisation and restructuring of SOEs. Handing over public activities to the private sector through asset sales or Public-Private Partnerships (PPPs) would contribute to developing the private sector, including SMEs, support growth activity and attract foreign investment.

Libya has gone through previous phases of privatisation, the latest between 2003 and 2008, during which 360 SOEs, ranging from small to large in various sectors, were either fully or partially privatised or brought in private partners through PPPs. Despite this, progress has been slow. Restrictions to individual shares and foreign ownership – individual investor's share of the capital was restricted to 15% and local ownership had to be at least 30% – resulted in limited interest in the privatisation programme.

A few high profile Initial Public Offerings (IPOs) were successful while many faltered. In most cases, disclosure about the assets for sale was shallow and the time given for due diligence insufficient, so that many assets had to be resubmitted to multiple rounds of bidding. In addition, there were several accusations of fraud, further discouraging investment. The PIB was appointed as the entity responsible for broadening ownership and matters related to privatisation, including the review of related regulatory policies. But a report by the Committee for Privatisation Programme Development in 2012 showed that the Board had not made any significant contribution.

Even if privatisation does eventually gain pace, a number of enterprises will remain under state ownership. These enterprises will need to be operated efficiently and in a competition-neutral manner or else they will act as a brake on SOE development through fiscal haemorrhaging and continued crowding out. As observed by LIAS (2014), "Addressing weak public sector management systems requires developing and implementing oversight mechanisms for transparency and accountability across all government institutions and state owned enterprises". Since many of these enterprises have traditionally been used as a source of employment and political patronage, the reform process will be very challenging.

Other countries have in the past taken a similar path. Their reform experience is embodied in OECD guidance documents and recommendations in this area which could also serve as guideposts for a Libyan reform process. The experience in the Western Balkans can provide useful lessons learned regarding privatisation efforts (Box 3.2) (Radulović and Dragutinović, 2015).

Box 3.2. **Privatisation examples in Western Balkans**

In Serbia, the privatisation of public companies had many difficulties dealing with ownership issues, absorbing redundant workers, and avoiding over indebtedness of the companies that were being privatised. These risks made it particularly challenging to find strategic investors able to transfer technology, conduct measures for operational restructuring and invest in the equipment (NALED, 2015).

The privatisation process in Montenegro highlights the importance of introducing mechanisms to prevent and fight corruption by amending relevant laws, and by introducing measures to increase transparency, public participation, and oversight over the privatisation processes (Zorica, 2015).

The case of Macedonia shows the importance of taking into account the institutional, economic, and political context when designing privatisation policies (Arsov, 2005). Analysis across 24 countries shows that successful privatisations go beyond a mere change of ownership and require broader complimentary reforms (IMF 2001). Strong institutions are need to address agency issues, ensure market competition, and depoliticise firm objectives among other factors.

3.10. Regulatory framework and business climate

A favourable business environment is critical to enabling a thriving private sector, including SMEs. In 2007, the General Planning Council established five committees to reform the commercial law, civil law, land law, labour law and court procedures (World Bank, 2011). After several piecemeal attempts at reforming the business law framework, the launch of major reforms in 2010 resulted in the amendment of several laws and enactment of new legislation. This included 22 new laws making fundamental changes relating to commercial activities, customs, income tax, the stock market, labour regulations and land registration. Further reforms were advanced by post-2011 governments, each one with a different ideological direction, creating uncertainty. Furthermore, instability in the country has impeded effective implementation of the new legislation. There are also deficiencies in some of the new regulations that should be addressed.

Business laws and regulations

The main laws regulating business activity in Libya are the commercial law, the civil law, the labour law, the investment promotion law, the free zone law and the banking law. The commercial law sets out the basic legal principles applied to commercial businesses and traders. Its enactment represented a significant update of the Commercial Law No. 9/1992 and replaced 90 other rules pertaining to commercial activities. The law is quite extensive and complex – it is 385 pages long and has 1 359 articles.[28]

Despite improvements, the new commercial law presents a number of shortcomings. It does not adequately cover several issues regarding the conclusion of commercial contracts, the settlement of commercial disputes and the protection of intellectual property. Commercial disputes are subject to litigation rules derived from the commercial law, but those rules apply to personal disputes and ignore the distinct nature of commercial disputes. Further amendments to the commercial law should take their distinct character of commercial disputes into account, rather than in a way akin to family- and civil-related disputes. Similarly, concluding a commercial contract involves applying the conditions and restrictions generally imposed on contracts as stipulated by the civil law, which is governed by the principle: "The contract is the law of the contracting parties". This principle is applied to all persons in all cases of commercial and civil disputes and requires great care on the part of companies in formulating their contracts to avoid difficulties in resolving later disputes.

A number of ministerial decrees issued after 2011 have modified the commercial law, creating uncertainty and concerns about future changes. These decrees have changed minimum capital requirements for joint venture companies, foreign ownership rules, restrictions on the number and shareholdings of investors, and limitations on the investment activities open to foreign companies (Box 3.3). These sometimes confusing and overlapping modifications have weighed heavily on investors' confidence, affecting their willingness to participate in projects.

Box 3.3. The legal structure of companies – a constantly changing landscape

Companies in Libya are governed by three pieces of legislation: *(1)* the commercial law;[a] *(2)* the investment law, which sets out the requirements to be met by an "investment enterprise"; and *(3)* Ministerial Decrees No. 03/2012 and No. 207/2012, regarding the participation of foreigners in joint venture companies and the opening of branches and representation offices for foreign companies in Libya. The interaction of the three creates confusion and unnecessary burden for Libyan and foreign investors wishing to start a company.

A joint venture company *(Mushtarika)* is a Libyan company with foreign participation allowed. This company form is often used by foreign investors and may carry on most types of activities, with exceptions of certain sectors reserved for Libyan nationals (e.g. retail trade, importation activities, catering services, land transport and shipping services, rock crushing and construction projects not exceeding LYD 30 million). Decree No. 103/2012 stated that foreigners could hold up to 65% of the shareholding capital of joint venture companies, but two months later the Ministry of Economy issued Decree No. 207/2012, reducing this to no more than 49%, which could be increased up to 60% with approval of the Ministry of Economy.[b] The new restriction was carried through to a new company law in 2013, which gave joint venture companies a certain timeframe to adjust their shareholdings to become compliant with the 49% rule, but since its passing the validity of the decree has been legally challenged. This led to Decree No. 22/2013, stating that the 49% ceiling does not apply to existing joint venture companies in Libya (IBP, 2014: 55).

In addition, Decree No. 103/2012 raised the minimum share capital of a *Mushtarika* company set up as a joint stock company to LYD 1 million (around USD 725 000). Given that the Libyan national now has to contribute more than 51% of the capital instead of 35%, the minimum amount he or she will need to bring is LYD 510 000 instead of LYD 350 000. So foreign investors find it less attractive to have a minority position in a joint venture, and Libyans will have a more difficult time raising the additional capital for their majority share, which could result in fewer development projects. The minority rule is also detrimental to newer and smaller Libyan ventures as many start-up ventures can no longer be capitalised to the same level by foreign investment partners as previously, thus putting them at a disadvantage in relation to the current economic elite of larger established businesses, which already control much of the private sector in Libya.[c] Decree No. 103/2012 also restricted limited liability companies to 100% ownership by Libyan nationals, which has implications for finance-constrained Libyan entrepreneurs.

Furthermore, Decree No. 186/2012 requires a minimum of ten shareholders in a joint stock company, with exceptions for public companies and under special circumstances. It also imposes the requirement that one shareholder cannot own more than 10% of the joint stock company's capital.[d] Since the Ministry of Economy stated that certain articles of Decree No. 207/2012 must be read in conjunction with Decree No. 186/2012, which reduces the shareholdings of any one investor, this means that foreign parties would not be able to benefit from even the 49% shareholding limit permitted by Decree No. 207/2012. Further obstacles would therefore be created for foreign investors.[e]

Investors, both national and foreign, also have the choice of establishing an investment enterprise under the investment law. These benefit from tax and customs duties exemptions and are most suitable for capital-intensive projects. The objective of the investment law is to encourage investment outside of the oil and gas sector to diversify the economy, so investment enterprises may operate in all major industry sectors, except upstream oil and gas. A foreign investor may wholly own the company if the foreign investment exceeds LYD 5 million. This is reduced to LYD 2 million if a Libyan partner holds at least half of the investment (IBP, 2014). In addition, investment enterprises can have a minimum number of two shareholders. It is not clear whether these provisions will be reversed under the Ministry of Economy Decree No. 186/2012, which would impose less flexibility.

Box 3.3. **The legal structure of companies – a constantly changing landscape** *(continued)*

The Ministry of Economy issued Decrees No. 103 and No. 207 in 2012, creating confusion regarding the allowable foreign investment limits. They also blur the previous separation between authorities and applicable legislation. In the past, the investment law was intended as a stand-alone law and the PIB was the sole authority for its implementation. Investment enterprises were approved by the PIB and issued an investment license; companies formed under the commercial law were regulated by the Ministry of Economy and issued a commercial license. Since the 2011 revolution, the Ministry of Economy is requiring investment enterprises to register for a commercial license, suggesting that the investment law must be interpreted in light of the more restrictive commercial law. The separation of the two laws and authorities should be clarified and possibly restored as previously.

Notes:

a. A chapter in the commercial law covers the different forms of companies, such as limited liability companies, limited partnership companies, joint stock companies, joint venture companies (involving Libyans with foreign partners). The terms of founding, managing and liquidating these companies are covered in a special chapter in the Libyan commercial law.

b. Decree 103/2012 was issued in May 2012.

c. "Libya: FDI In Libya: The Way" Clyde&Co, 17 July 2013: www.mondaq.com/x/251360/Corporate+Commercial+Law/FDI+In+Libya+The+Way/.

d. Decree 186/2012 was issued by the Ministry of Economy in April 2012.

e. See: "An overview of the current foreign investment laws and regulations in Libya", in *American Chamber of Commerce in Libya Newsletter,* Volume 1, Issue 2, June 2013.

Bankruptcy regulation

Libya does not have a separate bankruptcy law, but bankruptcy issues are covered under Articles 1012 and 1013 of the 2010 Commercial Law. According to this legislation, bankruptcy proceeds in two phases. The first is preventive reconciliation, during which the debtor attempts to rectify the financial situation of the business through an agreement with creditors under court supervision. The second phase commences in the event of the agreement's failure, whereby the court intercedes to protect the rights of the creditors through liquidation. The law should provide small enterprises with practical procedures regarding bankruptcy, including simplification of related litigation procedures and enabling creditors to collect their debts while encouraging small business owners to rectify their financial issues and return to their commercial activity as soon as possible.

Beyond legislation, there is no effective system in place, and there have been virtually no cases over the past five years involving a judicial reorganisation, judicial liquidation or debt enforcement procedure in Libya. For this reason Libya ranks last among 189 countries on the "resolving insolvency" indicator of the *Doing Business 2016* indicators (World Bank, 2016a).[29] Bankruptcy legislation also needs a judicial system that is effective in the expedient settlement of presented cases, bankruptcy experts and a competent executive system to carry out judicial sentences – all areas where Libya would benefit from improvements to expedite insolvency and bankruptcy proceedings and to give entrepreneurs who have failed a second chance to start a new business.

Competition laws

Policies to promote the entry of new businesses in a fair and competitive environment and provide the proper incentives for new and incumbent existing industry players to invest are essential for a dynamic business environment. When properly implemented they have a positive impact on investments (OECD, 2015b). This requires a sound and well-organised competition law, an effective competition authority that enforces the law and economic policies that respect the principles of competition and avoid restricting it unnecessarily (OECD, 2015b: 63). Competition mechanisms are particularly important for SMEs since they often suffer from high production costs and shortages in skilled labour and technology, making it extremely difficult to compete with large companies that receive investment concessions. The presence of many SOEs and a few large businesses that dominate much of the economic activity in Libya has impeded the entry of private Libyan businesses into many markets and stifled competition.

The commercial law introduced a competition framework for the first time. It calls for the establishment of a competition council and a supervisory board affiliated with the Ministry of Economy, which will be responsible for the law's execution and investigation of complaints, of noncompliance and violations. The competition provisions forbid all forms of market monopoly, applying to any case where dominant blocs control more than 30% of the market. Exceptions to this rule are subject to the approval of the minister of economy but apply to projects that support the reduction of production costs and are in the public interest or foster the transfer of technology and technical expertise and business opportunities that enhance competition for the benefit of microeconomic units.

The law signals a leap forward in protecting SMEs from unfair competition. But these provisions only apply to non-governmental commercial entities. More important, application of these provisions is virtually suspended as the competition council is yet to be established. Making the council operational to begin enforcing the competition laws will be imperative when a stable government is in place.

Administrative burdens for entry and growth

A favourable environment for the entry and operation of businesses requires rules that are easy to comply with. Reducing administrative burdens will decrease transaction costs for entrepreneurs and firms, increase the speed of setting up a company and boost the competitiveness of firms. Reducing the cost of registration and licensing is associated with higher levels of employment, productivity and firm creation, while excessive and cumbersome regulation for new enterprises is associated with higher levels of informality and corruption (Motta et al., 2010). Countries with weak business environments, such as Libya, require larger regulatory reforms in order to realise immediate gains in new firm registrations (Klapper and Love, 2011).

The 2011 conflict worsened the Libyan business environment, which was already characterised by complex administrative procedures under the previous regime. Regulatory uncertainty continues to pose a key challenge as businesses spend considerable time dealing with regulatory procedures that are often unclear and contradictory. Libya ranks 188 of 189 economies in the *Doing Business* index (World Bank, 2016a). It performs poorly in all indicators, and in dealing with construction permits, registering property and resolving insolvency it is considered a "no practice" country, meaning its institutions are not even functioning. Its performance in *Doing Business* indicators has deteriorated over the past two years, particularly in the per capita income cost of starting a business and of getting electricity.

Business registration procedures in Libya are lengthy and complex. Starting a business, which requires the use of lawyers, takes 10 steps and 35 days, compared to an average of 8.2 steps and 18.8 days in the MENA region (World Bank, 2016c). The process is much easier in neighbouring countries: 7 procedures and 8 days in Egypt, 4 procedures and 10 days in Morocco, 10 procedures and 11 days in Tunisia and 12 procedures and 20 days in Algeria. It costs 26.9% of per capita income, slightly more expensive than the MENA average, which is 25.8% of per capita income. The minimum capital requirement in Libya is 34.6% of per capita income, lower than the MENA average of 37.7% (World Bank, 2016c). However, 10 of the 20 MENA countries covered by the World Bank *Doing Business* report eliminated the minimum capital requirement, including Jordan, Egypt, Morocco and the United Arab Emirates.

The Ministry of Economy is the main institution for processing business registration requirements, including the issuing of certificates approving the business name, the type of business activity and incorporation documentation. These documents are submitted to the Tax Administration to register the company, following which the company must register with the Libyan Commercial Register in the Ministry of Economy and then obtain a company registration certificate at the commercial registry run by the Chamber of Commerce.

Before the 2011 revolution, a one-stop shop was established in Tripoli, with 22 regional offices. The mandate of the one-stop shop was to provide company registration certificates with access to all notaries. During and following the revolution, the management of the central company registry was disrupted, and the regional one-stop shops were forced to suspend their registry operations. As there is no national electronic company registry, all companies need to register in Tripoli, requiring notaries from other cities to travel to finalise the process. This creates additional business registration complexities and costs for entrepreneurs and investors living outside of Tripoli.

In addition, obtaining business licenses and permits is a lengthy process that can last several months. It requires the approval of a commission represented by multiple agencies, including the Social Security Administration, the Labour Administration, the Tax Administration, the Ministry of Interior and the Ministry of Economy. This can result in frequent and unpredictable delays and refusals (World Bank, 2011).

One of the first actions for Libya should be to re-open the regional one-stop shop offices. A possibility for easing co-ordination between agencies is for the one-stop shops to include officials from all entities involved in the business registration process, including the Ministry of Economy, the Tax Administration, the Social Security Administration and the Chamber of Commerce. Substantive reforms are required to simplify the process and procedures of reducing the time and cost of business registration and licensing.

Land and property rights

The recognition and protection of private property rights, secured through clear and fully enforced laws, is a crucial feature of a functioning market economy (Heritage Foundation, 2010). Secure property rights give entrepreneurs the confidence to invest in commercial project activity on a long-term basis, without fear of unfair expropriation or theft. Equally important, secure property rights are necessary for the financing of new and existing businesses, as property ownership provides a key source of collateral for securing bank loans.

For much of the Gaddafi regime, laws restricted the ownership of personal property. Many inconsistent laws about personal property rights were subsequently passed, giving rise to ambiguity and widespread conflict but resulting in limited private property ownership and weak protection of property rights. In principle, the state still retains the power, and reserves the right, to nationalise any property that has been privatised. Consequently, Libya earns a low property rights score of only 10 out of 100 in the *2016 Index of Economic Freedom* (Heritage Foundation, 2016).

Lands previously usurped by seizure, re-allocation or invasion by the state or individuals have kindled doubts over real estate property ownership, exacerbated by the lack of state enforcement of the law and spread of corruption. Post-2011 governments have pledged to return properties to their original owners, but this is proving to be a very difficult challenge. Besides the large number of claims that have been made, there is no clear law regulating land ownership and property rights. The Libyan cadastre, which provides complete registration of land ownership, has been closed since 2011, and the destruction of official property ownership documents in recent years has greatly complicated efforts to prove clear title to property throughout Libya. As a consequence of the ambiguity of property ownership, banks are reluctant to take property as collateral for loans until property ownership disputes are resolved, which is a serious issue for SMEs because land is the main source of collateral in Libya (OECD/EC/ETF, 2014).

Efforts must be exerted to reopen the Real Estate Register Office, provide alternative dispute resolution mechanisms for land disputes at a low cost and set a clear scheduled plan for compensating the original property owners. Timor-Leste can serve as example of a country where the property registration system was completely overhauled recently. Land records were destroyed in 1999, so when the country became independent in 2002 most of the land was occupied without official deeds, making land conflicts frequent. In 2007, a USAID-supported project started to regularise land ownership and cadastral surveys were conducted. By 2011, 91% of the land was covered by the surveys and the owners were allowed to obtain formal land titles.[30]

Tax obligations and administration

Corporate tax rates have in the past been subject to interpretation and negotiation between companies and Libyan tax authorities. Income Tax Law No. 7/2010 harmonised tax rates for domestic and foreign companies and reduced corporate rates to a flat tax of 20% of net profits.[31] However, implementation of this law has been impeded by the civil unrest.

The taxation law establishes procedural rules related to tax registration and collection. These apply equally to all kinds of commercial activities, whether freelance or individual work, co-operatives, partnerships, joint stock or limited liability companies. All businesses are required by law to register with the Tax Registry and provide a report on annual income certified by a chartered accountant. The law does not grant any special advantages to micro, small and medium enterprises, nor does it seek to reduce their tax-related administrative or financial burdens (in contrast to many OECD member countries). For example, the requirement to use the services of a chartered accountant poses an extra and costly burden on small businesses and may be one of the contributing factors in the high level of informality in the economy. This specific requirement should be reviewed for enterprises below a certain size.

Investment enterprises set up under the investment law are exempted from the new income tax law and continue to benefit from a five-year exemption from income tax, which, subject to approval, can be extended for an additional three years. This makes it very attractive to form investment enterprises.

Dealing with the Tax Administration itself can also be difficult. Tax filings are based on tax declarations following a deemed profit approach, according to the nature of the commercial activity.[32] This suggests that the ultimate tax cost determination can be open to a certain amount of subjectivity and uncertainty – and hence ripe for corruption practices. Complying with tax requirements in Libya is burdensome. According to the *Doing Business* indicators, it ranks 160 of 189 countries on the ease of paying taxes (World Bank, 2016b). A limited liability company in Libya would spend 889 hours a year dealing with taxation issues, compared to the average of 216 hours in the Middle East and North Africa. The government should reduce the compliance burden associated with tax administration, reducing time spent and helping businesses to become more productive.

Other weaknesses related to the taxation administration include widespread tax evasion, lack of tax awareness among businesses and absence of disclosure. Moreover, Libya does not have a database for tax registration and payer taxation numbers, and the administrative processes for estimating the amount of tax owed are outdated (computing is hardly used). Tax officials are rarely adequately trained and there is no clearly identified organisational structure.

3.11. Corruption

One of the biggest challenges as countries transform from central planning to market-based systems is to build transparent institutions and a corruption-free environment.[33] Corruption is a major deterrent to investment and business development as it increases the cost of doing business, prevents firms from operating on a level playing field and reduces confidence in government institutions.

The culture of corruption is deeply embedded in Libya, and it is widespread at all levels in the public administration (Mzioudet, 2014). The lack of transparency in the management of oil reserves and revenue, the issuance of government contracts and the enforcement of often ambivalent regulations has provided the government with many opportunities for rent-seeking and corruptive practices, with no accountability mechanisms.

Surveys of Libyans in 2006 reported various forms of corruption to be present across the country. These include: direct and indirect stealing and embezzlement of public money, nepotism and favouritism in employment, use of public resources for personal interest, kickbacks on trade contracts or purchases, bribe-taking in return for favours and money laundering as a means to evade the law (Transparency International, 2012).[34] According to Transparency International's 2013 survey, 46% of Libyan citizens felt the level of corruption in the country had increased "over the past two years", 53% that corruption in the public sector is a serious problem, with a high rate of bribery incidences, and 48% that government actions in the fight against corruption are ineffective.[35] "Corruption" and "inefficient government bureaucracy" were mentioned among the six most problematic factors for doing business in the *Global Competitiveness Report 2014-2015*, signalling weaknesses in the Libyan public administration impacting on business activities. Libya scores 16 out of 100 on the Corruption Perceptions Index 2015 and ranks 161 out of 168 countries (Transparency International, 2016) (Table 3.9).

Some efforts have been made to curb corruption, with different levels of success. For example, Libya's membership in the United Nations Convention Against Corruption (UNCAC)[36] has not translated into substantial anti-corruption actions or policies

(Transparency International, 2012). On the other hand, the National Audit Bureau, established to support financial transparency and limit corruption, has been continuously monitoring the work of government institutions; After the revolution, it was supported by civil society organisations (CSOs) serving as corruption watchdogs (Mzioudet, 2014). The bureau has also been publishing audit reports regarding the annual budgets of the Libyan government's financial institutions (e.g. the Libyan Sovereign Wealth Fund Institute). However, apart from the audit bureau, existing institutions have been arbitrary and ineffective with the application of anti-corruption measures. Worse, Gaddafi's patronage system has remained strong over the years.

Table 3.9. **High and persistent level of corruption perceptions in Libya**

	2015		2014	2013	2012
Country	**Rank/168**	**Score/100**	**Score/100**	**Score/100**	**Score/100**
Tunisia	76	38	40	41	41
Algeria	88	36	36	36	34
Egypt	88	36	37	32	32
Morocco	88	36	39	37	37
Libya	**161**	**16**	**18**	**15**	**21**
Average global score		**42.6**	**43.2**	**42.6**	**43.3**

Note: Score of 1 = highly corrupt; score of 100 = highly law-abiding.

Source: Corruption Perceptions Index 2015: www.transparency.org/cpi2015/#results-table.

The country needs to see significant institutional reforms that produce substantive results in the fight against corruption and towards improved governance standards. A national anti-corruption strategy should be developed. Libya would benefit from alignment with the OECD Anti-Bribery Convention, which focuses exclusively on bribery of public officials or international businesses. It would also benefit from more active participation in the Arab Anti-Corruption and Integrity Network (ACINET), in which the Libyan Ministry of Justice is a member. This would enable Libya to learn from regional exchange and policy dialogue, as well as access capacity building mechanisms.

The Libyan Transparency Association (LTA) was established in 2011 to curb corruption and promote the principles of transparency, good governance and accountability in business practices. It presented a draft law outlining the creation of a corruption authority, which would enforce penalties and implement transparency policies (Mzioudet, 2014). Civil society organisations such as the LTA have a key role to play in reshaping society and keeping the government accountable. The media and the private sector should be necessary partners in developing a national strategy to combat corruption.

While any efforts to strengthen institutions are currently derailed by the political instability and ongoing conflicts in the country, combating corruption should become a top priority of a unified government (Transparency International, 2016). This is needed to both build trust with citizens and create a more favourable business environment for private sector businesses.

In parallel, business integrity practices within the private sector are essential to reducing corruption and attracting foreign investors. In an environment that is deficient in its regulatory framework and rife with corruption practices, businesses will resort to participating in corruption (e.g. bribery, extortion, etc.) to facilitate their transactions with the government. Thus, in addition to implementing anti-corruption reforms, the government should promote business integrity practices within the private sector, such as codes of conduct and voluntary compliance programmes.

Assessing the potential risks for corruption in their business operations in a particular country is becoming a major factor that determines whether or not a company goes forward with an investment. Some MENA countries have adopted the OECD Guidelines for Multinational Enterprises or the OECD Convention on Combating Bribery of Foreign Public Officials in International Business Transactions – meaning that companies of those countries are bound by the standards. But most SMEs are either unaware of actions they can take to combat corruption or lack the necessary human and financial resources to develop sophisticated policies.

Active engagement in the MENA-OECD Business Integrity Network (MOBIN) would be beneficial to Libyans as it promotes the sharing of experiences and good practices in anti-corruption and integrity actions and assists in building national training capacities in business integrity practices, measures and tools (Box 3.4). The OECD Business Anti-Corruption Portal for SMEs operating in emerging and developing countries should be promoted among Libyan SMEs through business associations like chambers of commerce and the Libyan Business Council. They could also support the adoption of business integrity practices by raising awareness, sharing knowledge and experience and assisting with the establishment and implementation of corporate responsibility and integrity measures.

Box 3.4. MENA-OECD Business Integrity Network

Since 2011, the MENA-OECD Business Integrity Network (MOBIN) provides the business community with a unique channel for peer-learning and knowledge-sharing from the region and beyond in view of promoting better integrity standards and ethical business conduct. The network convenes business associations, private sector officials and experts in a public-private dialogue to discuss concrete ways to engage effectively in the fight against corruption, assess existing and innovative solutions to combat bribery and build up compliance approaches for companies.

The MOBIN engages with national, regional and multilateral partners to co-ordinate its activities. These include the General Confederation of Morocco Enterprises (Morocco), the Institut Arabe des Chefs d'Entreprise (Tunisia), the Egyptian Junior Business Association (Egypt), and the Center for International Private Enterprise and the United Nations Development Programme (UNDP) Project on Anti-Corruption and Integrity in the Arab Countries. The network seeks to achieve the following:

- support convergence of MENA regulatory frameworks and businesses with internationally recognised norms and standards
- provide an effective platform for public-private dialogue for peer-learning and sharing of tools and best practices
- promote mutual legal assistance and international co-operation in the detection, investigation and prosecution of complex corporate corruption cases.

Note: More information at www.oecd.org/mena/competitiveness/businessintegrityinthemiddleeastandnorthafrica.htm.

Annex 3.A1

Libyan stakeholder input on potential sectors – OECD Working Group 2015

Enterprise policies to develop new, productive sectors with a potential to gain a comparative advantage could eventually contribute to the Libyan export basket, and sector-driven value chain initiatives would increase productivity and promote integration of existing SMEs with multinational enterprises operating in the country. Economic diversification into higher value-added activities, characterised by higher wages and higher labour productivity would also reduce labour inefficiencies by creating incentives for young Libyans entering the labour market to join the productive private sector instead of turning to public employment.

The OECD carried out a sector analysis starting with an in-depth desk review analysis of sector trends and competitiveness in Libya. This analysis examined sector contribution to GDP, employment, labour productivity across sectors, exports and attractiveness for foreign direct investment (FDI). Consideration was also given to alignment of sector priorities with Libya's national development objectives and job creation impact. The OECD later carried out two rounds of stakeholder consultations in co-operation with Libya Enterprise to discuss the attractiveness, benefits and potential of an extensive preliminary list of sectors. Stakeholders held diverse views about the weights to be given to criteria for selecting sector priorities. For example, they considered labour intensive versus capital intensive and whether to take a short- versus long-term view on the development of sectors. They concurred the sectors should encompass products that are higher value added and exportable, and contribute to employment.

Stakeholders rated the list of sectors by sector attractiveness and country benefits criteria. The sectors considered to be the most attractive were construction materials and infrastructure, and petrochemicals. Education and training were considered as the highest in terms of country benefits and agri-business and renewable energies as very promising sectors with high growth potential.

Results of consultations and preliminary application of sector prioritisation framework

The full sector competitiveness analysis was presented and discussed at the OECD-Libya consultative meeting in July 2015. Pending further analysis, five priority sectors were generally agreed upon, largely consistent with the results of other studies of sector opportunities in Libya:

1. building and construction materials
2. ICTs
3. energy (renewables)

4. tourism/transit/logistics
5. agri-business, including fisheries opportunities.

When the political and security situation in Libya improves, the next step will be to develop sector road maps for each of the strategic priorities. These road maps will identify the market opportunities for the sector's products, the specific development needs of each sector, knowledge gaps, education and skills related to the sector, technical limitations, infrastructure needs, market structural barriers, regulatory limitations and other barriers to development of the sector. The road maps will further define the concrete actions needed to address the identified gaps and opportunities.

While trying to promote economic diversification and product sophistication, policies must ensure that they do not distort the economy and give unfair advantages to certain businesses. Businesses must not be allowed to abuse their market power or be given an opportunity for rent-seeking and the creation of entrenched privileges. Consequently, sector diversification policies need to be monitored carefully.

	Sector attractiveness				Country benefits	
Sectors/sub-sectors	Industry size	Export size	FDI attraction	Labour capital intensity	Alignment with national strategy	Impact on job creation
Services						
ICT	L	L	L	L	M	M
Transit trade (ports, shipping, marine services)	M	M	L	M	M	H
Tourism (and value chain)	L	M	M	M	H	H
Transportation	L	L	M	M	H	M
Education and training	M	L	M	H	H	H
Health services	M	M	H	M	M	M
Financial services	H	L	H	M	H	M
Industry and mining						
Agri-business (including food processing)	M	M	H	M	M	M
Renewable energies	L	M	H	M	M	M
Construction materials and infrastructure	H	L	H	H	M	H
Petrochemicals	H	H	H	M	H	L
Recycling	L	L	M	M	L	M

Note: Participants graded variables high (H), medium (M) and low (L) for each sub-sector.

Source: OECD (2013a), "Joint OECD/Libya Mission, Mission Report", Tripoli, 8 to 12 September, p. 21.

Sector strengths

Sector	Strengths
Energy	• Competitive sector with greatest potential to become a strategic sector for the Libyan economy. • The petrochemicals sub-sector produces some products that appear as emerging product champions. • Renewable energies (wind and solar) is a growing sector for which demand is expected to increase in the future. Moreover, there is a favourable climate for solar energy. • High potential to attract domestic and foreign investment.
Agro-food and agro-chemicals	• Food processing is very promising, but the focus should be on a specific set of products, given the scarcity of arable land (e.g. olives and palm olives, dates and natural herbs). The sub-sector also needs reforms to develop and to be able to compete with foreign products. • Fisheries is a competitive sector in Libya, but it may not represent a strategic sector in the longer run as resources may be limited and the capacity to offer jobs in line with the qualifications and expectations of Libyan nationals may be relatively weak. • Potential in animal products factories, salt lakes, precious stones and minerals.
Construction materials and equipment	• Many construction materials currently imported could be replaced by Libyan products because in many cases the material is available in the country (e.g. concrete, iron and steel). The sector needs to be privatised to be more competitive. • Cement refineries have promising potential, and cement factories are privatised by up to 70%. • The steel industry has some potential to develop and gain in competitiveness.
ICT sector	• Substantial existing demand for basic ICT services that could serve as a foundation for further growth. • High future demand and strong potential as internet penetration is still extremely low. • Increasing number of graduates in relevant fields makes for an ample supply of human capital. • Low entry barriers for many parts of the sector. • Poor telecommunications infrastructure remains a major constraint, plus the ICT sector is largely dominated by the public sector and not competitive. The privatisation of ICT services would foster the development of the sector, but a number of actions are needed to integrate the private enterprises into this sector (e.g. a telecommunications law and the establishment and operationalisation of a regulatory body).
Transport and logistics	• Transit trade is very promising due to the strategic location of Libya in the region. Transport hubs like Tripoli and Sabha already exist, and Misrata has a transit zone, although it is not yet very dynamic. • Transit hubs could be supplemented by special economic zones or free zones. • Public transport has development potential, especially for creating jobs. Some 100 planned projects were signed by the government as part of the development plan for 2008-12, many of which are still to be implemented.
Tourism	• The Ministry of Tourism has already drafted a tourism strategy and identified 12 promising locations. • Substantial opportunity for growth to catch up with neighbouring countries. • Attractive sector for FDI. • Would need substantial co-ordinated investments along the value chain.
Education and training sectors	• Higher value added is needed. • Better wages. • Fit with the skills needed by the economy.
Other potential promising sectors	• Repair and maintenance (cars, housing, etc.) • Retail trade • Health services • Recycling • Financial services

Sources: OECD (2014), "Consultative meeting for the diagnostic study – Meeting Summary" 25-26 September; OECD (2013b), "SME Development Strategy Project for Libya, Joint OECD/Libya Mission, Mission Report", Tripoli, Libya – 8 to 12 September.

Findings of other studies on priority sectors for Libya's development

Several previous studies assessed the sector competitiveness of the Libyan economy. The Libyan Institute of Planning and the Monitor Group (2006) identified agriculture, construction, energy, tourism and financial services as the most promising and competitive sectors of the Libyan economy. In a study prepared for the Libyan National Economic Development Board (NEBD), the Korean Institute for Development Strategy (KDS) classified strategic priority sectors according to two variables: market potential (demand) and national competitiveness (supply) (KDS, 2010). The KDS adopted a long-term perspective, which may not always correlate with sectors that are expected to be growing strongly in the short term. The study identified five strategic or priority sectors:

1. energy: oil and gas, petrochemical, metal processing, renewables
2. construction: engineering, construction, construction materials and equipment
3. hospitality and tourism: restaurants, hotels, resorts and entertainment, social care and social work
4. ICT: software development, system integration, database management and network management
5. repair and maintenance: autos, garments, buildings and infrastructure.

The KDS (2010) study attempts to match the corresponding types of jobs demanded by the five strategic sectors to employment promotion policies and skills development. It recommends the preparation of national development plans for these strategic sectors, as well as the elaboration and implementation of related employment promotion plans and programmes.

The GIZ (2009) study ranks sectors according to their growth potential, based on the perceptions of general managers from the Libyan private sector. Construction, energy and energy-dependent industries, trade, ICT and transport were perceived as the most dynamic sectors. Financial services and insurance, health services, agriculture and manufacturing were perceived as the least dynamic sectors.

The Altai Consulting (2013) study assessed sector competitiveness or attractiveness in the cities of Benghazi and Misrata. Based on interviews with private sector representatives and businesses, the findings suggest that the most dynamic sectors in 2012 were domestic private construction (driven, inter alia, by an easing of building regulations) and the trade sector. Manufacturing was perceived to be performing to some extent better than before 2011, with building materials and food processing as the most promising activities in the longer term. The study recommended mapping and assessing "supply chain and service needs in Libya's food and building materials manufacturing sub-sectors" and also identifying areas where Libyan supply chain inputs (e.g. packaging and raw materials) or services (e.g. cleaning and distribution) could replace foreign intermediaries or services. Finally, the study identified opportunities in ICT and private healthcare services as erratic and limited due to strong regional competition.

The World Bank has identified sector growth opportunities for Libya and implications for private sector and SME development (Calice et al., 2015), making the following observations:

- Substantial growth in the trade sector since 2011 due to high demand for imported products and the rise of private supermarkets, grocery stores and clothing retailers. The majority of this growth has come from the private sector and is expected to continue in a post-conflict environment. This will also create demand for more manufactured food products and elevate that sector as one with growth potential.

- When the situation improves, the construction sector is likely to drive a large share of Libya's growth due to the high demand for new housing, reconstruction, anticipated metro, railway and other infrastructure projects. The construction sector is also attractive because it creates demand for building materials and jobs for highly-skilled workers, as well as sub-contracting opportunities for SMEs.
- The real estate sector (e.g. hotel investments, resorts, shopping malls, apartment complexes) is a strong sector for future expansion, with anticipated growth in 2015 50% higher than in 2014. Small firms are unlikely to be direct players in real estate projects because of the large capital investment required, but many of the projects have the potential for significant job creation and supplier opportunities for domestic SMEs (e.g. resort complexes). In addition, the sector is attractive to foreign investors.
- Although the private healthcare and education sectors are small contributors to output value at the present time, they have growth potential in the future. Private health centres (e.g. clinics and pharmacies) represent an estimated 40% of the health market, and private services grew by 60% in 2012, 30% in 2013 and about 5% in 2014. The sector has a number of value chain spillovers, creating demand for medical equipment importers, diagnostic laboratories, ambulance services, and medical training centres, which also could create opportunities for SMEs. The education system was closed to private establishments during the 70s-90s. Since then the number of private schools, colleges and universities has been expanding rapidly, with an estimated enrolment of 100 000 students by the end of 2013 and output value of USD 125 million in 2014.
- The tourism sector is underdeveloped and likely to remain limited until the security situation improves. Restaurants, cafes and catering businesses have been growing rapidly in larger cities. This sub-sector has significant job-creating potential, as well as for entrepreneurial start-ups.
- The transport and shipping sector has private sector and SME development potential, primarily because it facilitates the distribution system for imports and exports. As demand increases for the movement of consumer goods, raw materials, production equipment, exports, as well as people, so will the opportunities for new businesses to enter the market to meet the expanding needs. Although the output value of the sector is currently relatively small (estimated USD 370 million in 2014), it can be expected to grow significantly in the future – in line with the transit hub vision of previous governments.
- The food manufacturing sector is expected to grow, which will create opportunities for SMEs to produce food products for domestic markets (including import replacement) and exports (e.g. dates, olive oil, fish), as well in the value chain of packaging, distribution, waste management and other ancillary services.

The World Bank suggested that the sectors with the strongest short-term and long-term employment potential are in construction, manufacturing, wholesale and retail trade, agriculture/fishery, hospitality and services (Elgazzar et al., 2015), which is in line with the World Bank's sector growth predictions (Calice et al., 2015).

Notes

1. OECD calculation based on data from the Central Bank of Libya and the General Information Authority. Following McMillan and Rodrik (2011), the measure of productivity gaps is calculated by dividing labour productivity in each sector by average labour productivity.

2. Revealed Comparative Advantage is an expression of the share of a commodity in one country's total exports divided by the sum of the shares of this same commodity in other countries' total exports (in a region or worldwide) (Balassa, 1965). Products with a ratio of 1 or more are considered to have a Revealed Comparative Advantage; the higher the RCA, the more competitive the product is in international markets. The more diversified a country is (number of products exported with a RCA>1) and the more exclusive the goods it exports, the more complex the productive structure is and the higher its growth prospects (Hidalgo and Hausmann, 2009). Export diversification, which evaluates the level of changes in the composition of a country's export mix, is often used as a measure of economic diversification because several empirical studies have shown it to be a key explanatory variable of economic growth in a large panel of economies (Al-Marhubi, 2000; and Berthélemy and Söderling, 2001).

3. Findings show that the more economies are diversified and at the same time produce uncommon products that few countries export, the higher levels of GDP per capita they display.

4. "Country at a Glance", World Bank (www.worldbank.org/en/country/libya/overview/).

5. "CBL warns 2015 budget deficit up to LD 30 bn, recommends firm reform measures", *Libya Herald*, 4 April, 2015, https://www.libyaherald.com/2015/04/04/cbl-warns-2015-budget-deficit-up-to-ld-30-bn-recommends-firm-reform-measures/.

6. The score value was 3.2/7.0 in 2010-2011 and 1.9/7.0 in 2014-2015.

7. World Development Indicators database, October 2015 edition.

8. The employment to population ratio uses the population 15+ years as the base.

9. World Development Indicators Database, October 2015 edition, World Bank.

10. Elgazzar et al. (2015) cite estimates provided by the Bureau of Statistics and Census and the Libyan Ministry of Labour.

11. According to Ministry of Finance statistics, in April 2013 the government was paying salaries to 1.5 million public employees, about 80% of all employment. The size of the public sector has further increased during the last three years, along with an increase in the amount of wages and subsidies (OECD, 2014). In particular, public sector hiring increased and wages doubled during the revolution.

12. The high level of employment in the public sector is similar to other resource-rich economies in the MENA region. For example, 87% of Qatar nationals are employed in the public sector, 86% in Kuwait and 72% in Saudi Arabia (IMF, 2013). However, Libya does not compare favourably with other economies of the region, such as Egypt, which has 25% in public sector employment, or Morocco, with 14% (Assaad, 2013).

13. "A high value of domestic credit to private sector (% of GDP) is a sign of a strong economy!" https://ecohorizons.wordpress.com/2014/09/22/713/.

14. Libya ranks 144 of 144 countries and has a score of 1.95 of 7.

15. Non-performing loans at the end of 2012 were 21% of total loans (IMF, 2013: 5).

16. www.fdiattractiveness.com/ranking-2014/.

17. Alfituri (2013) cite this data from the 2010 Annual Report of the Ministry of Economics, Trade and Investment Libya.

18. Restrictions include requiring a minimum of 10 shareholders in a joint stock company, limiting the shareholding of any one investor to no more than 10%, restricting the foreign participation

in a joint stock company to no more than 49%, disallowing joint venture companies between foreigners and Libyans to operate in a number of sector activities and prohibiting the establishment of limited liability companies by foreigners.

19. A sovereign fund whose aim is to diversify national sources of revenue and incentivise the private sector, especially SMEs that are also engaged in promoting partnerships between Libyan and foreign enterprises.

20. Crude oil, refined oil products, natural gas and chemical compounds.

21. World Development Indicators database, October 2015 edition, World Bank.

22. World Development Indicators database, October 2015 edition, World Bank. In 2013, transport services rose to 73% of all services exports (there is no 2013 data for travel services).

23. The LPI is determined on the basis of in-country interviews and reflects perceptions of a country's logistics. This includes the efficiency of customs and border clearance processes, the quality of trade- and transport-related infrastructure, the ease of arranging competitively priced shipments, the competence and quality of logistics services (e.g. trucking, freight forwarding, customs brokerage), the ability to track and trace consignments and the frequency with which shipments reach the consignee within the scheduled time (i.e. timeliness) (http://data.worldbank.org/indicator/LP.LPI.OVRL.XQ/).

24. The IPRI aims to quantify the strength of both physical and intellectual property rights and rank countries accordingly.

25. U.S. Department of State, "2014 Investment Climate Statement – Libya", www.state.gov/e/eb/rls/othr/ics/2014/230690.htm.

26. U.S. Department of State, "2014 Investment Climate Statement – Libya", www.state.gov/e/eb/rls/othr/ics/2014/230690.htm.

27. "Enterprise skills, entrepreneurial learning, and innovation in SMEs in Libya", presentation by Dr. Dia Eddin Sadek Abuhadra at the OECD Consultative meeting for the diagnostic study: SME Development Strategy Project for Libya, Istanbul, 29-30 July 2015.

28. The commercial law covers a broad range of issues related to commercial agency, brokerage, commercial contracts and commercial obligations, business contracting, transport contracts, commercial mortgages, banking operations, commercial bonds, bankruptcy, competition, protection of consumer rights, the Chambers of Commerce and Industry and Agriculture, the General Union of Chambers of Commerce and companies.

29. It is considered a "no practice" country for this indicator.

30. USAID, www.usaidlandtenure.net/sites/default/files/country-profiles/full-reports/USAID_Land_Tenure_Timor-Leste_Profile.pdf.

31. Tax regulations of 2006 were to some extent size-sensitive in that tax on businesses with no more than 50 employees could not exceed LYD 2.5 million. Such a provision was removed in the new 2010 tax law.

32. Taxable deemed profit ranges from 10% to 40% of revenue, e.g. 12%-20% of revenue for construction businesses, 18%-25% for services businesses, 25%-40% for design, consulting and engineering businesses, and 5%-8% of revenue for supply businesses (Amereller, 2014).

33. OECD, "Practices to Strengthen Business Integrity in the MENA Region", www.oecd.org/mena/competitiveness/PracticesBusinessIntegrity.pdf.

34. Based on results of an uncited study carried out in 2007 by the Organization for Transparency in Libya.

35. Global Corruption Barometer 2013 database (www.transparency.org/gcb2013/in_detail/).

36. The UNCAC calls for both preventive and punitive anti-corruption measures and provides guidance to governments and businesses working to promote transparency, integrity and accountability.

References

AfDB/OECD/UNDP (2015), *African Economic Outlook 2015: Regional Development and Spatial Inclusion*, OECD Publishing, Paris, http://dx.doi.org/10.1787/aeo-2015-en.

AfDB/OECD/UNDP (2014), *African Economic Outlook 2014, Regional Edition: North Africa*, OECD Publishing, Paris.

Alfituri, A. (2013), "The Libyan Experience of Foreign Direct Investment", *South East Africa Journal of Contemporary Business, Economics and Law*, Vol. 2(2).

Al-Marhubi, F. (2000), "Export diversification and growth: an empirical investigation", *Applied Economics Letters*, 7(9): 559–562.

Amereller (2014), "Doing Business in Libya: Opportunities and Challenges of the Transition", November, Amereller Legal Consultants, Tripoli.

Arsov (2005), "Post-Privatisation Retrospective of Macedonia – Could We Have Done it Better?", Peter Lang, Frankfurt am Mein, S. Kusic (editor), 2005.

Assaad, R. (2013), "Making Sense of Arab Labor Markets: The Enduring Legacy of Dualism", IZA Discussion Paper Np. 7573, Institute for the Study of Labor (IZA), Bonn.

Balassa, B. (1965), "Trade Liberalisation and "Revealed Comparative Advantage", *The Manchester School*, Vol. 33(2): 99–123.

Bälz, K. and P. Greco (2014), "Libya: Law No. 1 of 2013 on the prohibition of interest-based financing transactions", in *Banking Law Newsletter*, February, International Bar Association Legal Practice Division, Amereller Legal Consultants, Munich.

Barro, R.J. and J.W. Lee (2013), "A new data set of educational attainment in the world, 1950–2010*"*, *Journal of Development Economics*, Elsevier, Vol. 104: 184–198.

Berthélemy, J. C. and L. Söderling (2001), "The role of capital accumulation, adjustment and structural change for economic take-off: Empirical evidence from African growth episodes", *World Development*, 29(2), 323–343.

Braun, G. (2011), "Improving the Quality of Basic and Specialised Secondary Education in Libya", Abridged Version Labour Market Study: Competencies for Development – A New Role for Education, GIZ/International Services, Eschborn.

Calice, P., T. Benattia, A. Carriere and E. Davin (2015), *Simplified Enterprise Survey and Private Sector Mapping: Libya 2015*, World Bank Group, Washington, DC, http://documents.worldbank.org/curated/en/2015/09/25016718/simplified-enterprise-survey-private-sector-mapping-libya-2015.

Chauffour, J-P. (2013), *From Political to Economic Awakening in the Arab World: The Path of Economic Integration - Deauville Partnership Report on Trade and Foreign Direct Investment*, World Bank, Washington, DC.

Clark N. (2013), *Education in a Transitional Libya*, World Education News & Reviews, http://wenr.wes.org/2013/07/education-in-a-transitional-libya/.

CMI (Center for Mediterranean Integration) (2013), *Transforming Arab Economies: Traveling the Knowledge and Innovation Road*, Prepared in co-operation with the European Investment Bank (EIB), the World Bank, and the Islamic Educational, Social, and Cultural Organization (IESCO), World Bank, Washington, DC.

Commission of the European Communities (2008), "'Think Small First', A 'Small Business Act' for Europe", Communication from the Commission to the Council, the European Parliament, the European Economic and Social Committee and the Committee of the Regions, European Commission, Brussels.

Crisp, W. (2013), "Libya's banks struggle to escape Gaddafi's shadow", *EuroMoney*, www.euromoney.com/Article/3211071/Libyas-banks-struggle-to-escape-Gaddafis-shadow.html.

Dempsey, M. (2013), *Libya in Transition: Reforming the financial sector to spur economic growth*, in association with Brehon Advisory, Legatum Institute, London.

Efhialelbum, A. and P. Flatau (2013), "Did Foreign Direct Investment Contribute to the Libyan Economic Growth in Transition Period?", *Mediterranean Journal of Social Sciences*, Vol. 4(9): 46–55, DOI: 10.5901/mjss.2013.v4n9p46/.

Elgazzar, H., A.R. Lahga, M.B.N. Quota, F.U. Rother and L. Hargreaves (2015), *Labor Market Dynamics in Libya: Reintegration for Recovery*, World Bank Group, Washington, DC., http://documents.worldbank.org/curated/en/2015/06/24650277/labor-market-dynamics-libya-reintegration-recovery.

Elmansori, E. and L. Arthur (2014), "Obstacles to Innovation Faced by Small and Medium Enterprises (SMEs) in Libya", *International Journal of Innovation and Knowledge Management in Middle East & North Africa (IJIKMMENA)*, Vol. 2(1), World Association for Sustainable Development (WASD), London.

ETF (European Training Foundation) (2014), *Labour Market and Employment Policy in Libya*, European Training Foundation, Torino.

G8/UK Presidency Deauville Partnership (2013), "Action Plan for Investment Reform Priorities in Libya", London.

Gelb, A. (2011), "Economic diversification in resource rich countries", in Arezki, R., T. Gylfason and A. Sy (eds.), *Beyond the curse: Policies to harness the power of natural resources*, International Monetary Fund, Washington, DC.

Hausmann, R., C.A. Hidalgo, S. Bustos, M. Coscia, A. Simones and M.A. Yildirim (2013), *The Atlas of Economic Complexity: Mapping Paths to Prosperity*, MIT Press, Cambridge.

Hausmann, R. and S. Bustos (2012), "Structural transformation in Egypt, Morocco, and Tunisia: A comparison with China, South Korea, and Thailand", in *Comparative study on export policies in Egypt, Morocco, Tunisia and South Korea*, African Development Bank, Tunis.

Hausmann, R., J. Hwang and D. Rodrik (2007), "What you export matters", *Journal of Economic Growth*, 12(1), 1–25.

Heritage Foundation (2016), *2016 Index of Economic Freedom: Promoting Economic Opportunity and Prosperity*, Heritage Foundation and Wall Street Journal, Washington, DC.

Heritage Foundation (2012), *2012 Index of Economic Freedom: Promoting Economic Opportunity and Prosperity*, Heritage Foundation and Dow Jones & Company, Washington, DC.

Heritage Foundation (2010), *2010 Index of Economic Freedom: Promoting Economic Opportunity and Prosperity*, Heritage Foundation and Dow Jones & Company, Washington, DC.

Hidalgo, C.A. and R. Hausmann (2009), "The building blocks of economic complexity", *Proceedings of the National Academy of Sciences*, 106(26), 10570–10575.

Hidalgo, C.A. et al. (2007), "The product space conditions the development of nations", *Science*, 317(5837), 482–487.

Ianchovichina, E. and M. Burger (2013), *Middle East and North Africa - Economic developments and prospects 2013: Investing in turbulent times*, World Bank Group, Washington, DC, http://documents.worldbank.org/curated/en/2013/10/18843310/mena-economic-developments-prospects-2013-investing-turbulent-times.

Ianchovichina, E., L. Mottaghi and S. Devarajan (2015), *Inequality, uprisings, and conflict in the Arab World*, Middle East and North Africa (MENA) Economic Monitor, World Bank Group, Washington, DC, http://documents.worldbank.org/curated/en/2015/10/25119063/inequality-uprisings-conflict-arab-world.

IBP (2014), "Libya Company Laws and Regulations Handbook", *International Business Publications*, Washington, DC.

IMF (2016), "Economic Diversification in Oil-Exporting Arab Countries", Annual Meeting of Arab Ministers of Finance.

IMF (2015), *World Economic Outlook: Adjusting to Lower Commodity Prices*, October, International Monetary Fund, Washington, DC.

IMF (2013), "Libya 2013 Article IV Consultation", IMF Country Report No. 13/150, International Monetary Fund, Washington, DC.

IMF (2001), "The Gains from Privatization in Transition Economies: Is "Change of Ownership" Enough?", Staff Papers Vol. 48, Special Issue, International Monetary Fund, Washington, DC.

Jarreau, J. and S. Poncet (2012), "Export sophistication and economic growth: Evidence from China", *Journal of Development Economics*, 97(2), 281–292.

KDS (Korea Institute for Development Strategy) and KOREATECH (Korea University of Technology and Education) (2013), *Preparation of a Master Plan for the National Development and Implementation of Labor Market Information System for Employment Promotion in Libya*, Ministry of Strategy and Finance, Seoul.

Klapper, L. and I. Love (2011), "The Impact of Business Environment Reforms on New Firm Registration", Policy Research Working Paper 5493, World Bank, Washington, DC.

LIAS (Libya Institute for Advanced Studies) (2014), *Libya 2020 Vision*, Libya Institute for Advanced Studies, Tripoli.

Lo Turco, A. and D. Maggioni (2015), "On firms' product space evolution: the role of firm and local product relatedness", *Journal of Economic Geography*.

McMillan, M.S. and D. Rodrik (2011), "Globalization, structural change and productivity growth", No. w17143, National Bureau of Economic Research, Cambridge.

Mishra, S., S. Lundström and R. Anand (2011), "Service export sophistication and economic growth", Policy Research Working Papers, World Bank, Washington, DC.

Mo Ibrahim Foundation (2015), "2015 Ibrahim Index of African Governance: Executive Summary", Mo Ibrahim Foundation, London.

Monitor Group (2006), *National Economic Strategy: An Assessment of the Competitiveness of the Libyan Arab Jamahiriya*, General Planning Council of Libya, Tripoli.

Motta, M., A.M. Oveido and M. Santini (2010), "An Open Door for Firms: The Impact of Business Entry Reforms," Viewpoint 323, World Bank Group, Washington, DC.

Mzioudet, H. (2014), "Libya's Other War: Fighting Corruption for Sustainable Stability – Attempts at curbing Libya's culture of corruption", Sadeq Institute, Tripoli, www.sadeqinstitute.org/wp-content/uploads/2014/10/Libyas-Other-War.pdf.

NALED (2015), "Cases Studies of Privatization in Serbia", National Alliance for Local Economic Development.

OECD (forthcoming), *Special Economic Zones: Helping resource-rich countries diversify*, OECD, Paris.

OECD (2015a), *Russian Federation: Key Issues and Policies,* OECD Studies on SMEs and Entrepreneurship, OECD Publishing, Paris, http://dx.doi.org/10.1787/9789264232907-6-en.

OECD (2015b), *The Policy Framework for Investment*, 2015 Edition, OECD, Paris, http://dx.doi.org/10.1787/9789264208667-en.

OECD (2014), "SME Development Strategy Project for Libya: Consultative meeting for the diagnostic study - Meeting Summary", OECD, Paris.

OECD (2013a), *Interconnected Economies: Benefiting from Global Value Chains*, OECD Publishing, Paris, http://dx.doi.org/10.1787/9789264189560-en.

OECD (2013b), *SME Development Strategy Project for Libya*, OECD, Tripoli.

OECD (2012), *OECD Science, Technology and Industry Outlook 2012*, OECD Publishing, Paris, http://dx.doi.org/10.1787/sti_outlook-2012-en.

OECD (1997), *Diffusing Technology to Industry: Government Policies and Programmes*, OECD Publishing, Paris.

OECD, EC (European Commission), and ETF (European Training Foundation) (2014), *SME Policy Index: The Mediterranean* Middle East and North Africa 2014: Implementation of the "Small Business Act for Europe, OECD Publishing, Paris.

Property Rights Alliance (2015), *International Property Rights Index 2015 Report*, Americans for Tax Reform Foundation/Property Rights Alliance, Washington, DC.

Radulović, B. and Dragutinović, S. (2015), *Case studies of privatizations in Serbia*, National Alliance for Local Economic Development, Belgrade.

Schwab, K. (2014), *The Global Competitiveness Report 2014–2015*, World Economic Forum, Geneva.

Schwab, K. (2013), *The Global Competitiveness Report 2013–2014*, World Economic Forum, Geneva.

Schwab, K. (2010), *The Global Competitiveness Report 2010–2011*, World Economic Forum, Geneva.

Transparency International (2016), *Corruption Perceptions Index 2015*, Transparency International, Berlin.

Transparency International (2012), "Corruption Trends in the Middle East and North Africa Region (2007–2011)", U4 Anti-Corruption Resource Centre, Transparency International, Berlin, http://www.u4.no/publications/corruption-trends-in-the-middle-east-and-north-africa-region-2007-2011/.

Troug, H.A. and R. Sbia (2015), "The Relationship between Banking Competition and Stability in Developing Countries: The Case in Libya", *International Journal of Economic and Financial Issues*, Vol. 5(3): 772–779.

UNDP (2015), *Human Development Report 2015: Work for Human Development*, United Nations Development Programme, New York.

Upper Quartile (2013), "Review of Workstream 3 – Job Centres", December, Libyan Private Sector Development Institutions (LPSDI), Upper Quartile, Edinburg.

Wahab, K.A. and K.H. Abdesamed (2012), "Small and Medium Enterprises (SMEs) Financing Practice and Accessing Bank Loan Issues -The Case of Libya", *International Journal of Social, Behavioral, Educational, Economic, Business and Industrial Engineering*, Vol. 6(12): 3715–3720.

WJP (World Justice Project) (2015), *Rule of Law Index 2015*, World Justice Project, Washington, DC.

World Bank (2016a), *Doing Business 2016: Measuring Regulatory Quality and Efficiency*, 13th Edition, World Bank, Washington, DC.

World Bank (2016b), *Doing Business 2016: Measuring Regulatory Quality and Efficiency - Economy Profile 2016 Libya,* World Bank, Washington, DC.

World Bank (2016c), *Doing Business 2016: Regional Profile 2016 Middle East and North Africa (MENA),* World Bank, Washington, DC.

World Bank (2015a), *Labour Market Dynamics in Libya: Reintegration for Recovery, Libya 2015,* World Bank, Washington, DC.

World Bank (2015b), *Simplified Enterprise Survey and Private Sector Mapping, Libya 2015,* World Bank, Washington, DC.

World Bank (2015c), *2015 World Development Indicators*, World Bank, Washington, DC.

World Bank (2014a), *Connecting to Compete: Trade Logistics in the Global Economy – The Logistics Performance Index and its Indicators*, World Bank, Washington, DC.

World Bank (2014b), "Promoting Foreign Investment in Fragile and Conflict-Affected Situations", *Investment Promotion in Practice*, No. 22, World Bank, Washington, DC.

World Bank (2013), "Programmatic Approach for ESW/TA Concept Note: Supporting Finance and Private Sector Development in Libya", World Bank, Washington, DC.

World Bank (2012), *World Development Report 2013: Jobs*, World Bank, Washington, DC.

World Bank (2011), "Libya Investment Climate: Enhancing Private Sector Performance for Diversification and Employment", World Bank, Washington, DC. Unpublished.

Zorica (2015), "Privatisation in Montenegro – Highway to Destitution", German Federal Foreign Office, Munich.

Chapter 4

Libya's SME policies

This chapter examines SME and entrepreneurship policies in Libya, including the institutional framework and programmes. It analyses co-ordination mechanisms, business support services and financing and initiatives. While the government has initiated several policy measures and programmes to bolster the SME sector – such as financial assistance and programmes to support start-ups through entrepreneurship training, information and advice – the review identifies a number of policy gaps. Broader and deeper measures and enhanced institutional structures are needed. The chapter also highlights opportunities for development of sectors that could lead to greater diversification of the economy outside the hydrocarbon sector and future growth of the SME sector.

4.1. Institutional framework

SME and entrepreneurship policies in Libya are relatively nascent. The 2006 Economic Development Strategy included SME promotion as a mechanism to "catalyse innovation, risk-taking and business formation in Libya, and create the next generation of Libyan entrepreneurs" (General Planning Council of Libya, 2006: 66). The 2030 Vision Committee plan focuses on SME promotion as one of its main components to drive the economy forward.

In 2007, the National Economic Development Board (NEDB) was established and the National SME Programme launched. The SME Programme was comprehensive, and it was aligned with principles proposed by the OECD and the European Commission.[1] The programme can be further refined, as it does not address the specific challenges faced by young entrepreneurs, women entrepreneurs, ethnic minorities or regional disparities. But some progress has been made. For example, business incubators and enterprise centres have been established in certain parts of the country.

Main institutions

There are several institutions dealing with SME policies in Libya. Three ministries have been involved in some aspect of enterprise development since the revolution: the Ministry of Economy, the Ministry of Industry and the Ministry of Labour and Manpower. The Libyan Programme for Reintegration and Development (LPRD, previously the Warriors Affairs Commission) within the prime minister's office also works on SME development.[2]

In 2007, an agency called the National SME Programme was created under the Economic Development Council within the Prime Minister's Office. In 2012, it was renamed as Libya Enterprise and re-established under the Ministry of Economy. Libya Enterprise guides SMEs and leads the National SME Programme. It is overseen by an SME steering committee, headed by the second deputy prime minister and composed of the ministers of economy, planning, labour, industry, finance and the heads of Libya Enterprise and the LPRD. This committee is in charge of developing Libya Enterprise's strategies and plans for SME development, including following up on their funding.

Libya Enterprise's mandate is to promote entrepreneurship, create a supportive environment for SMEs, establish enterprise centres and incubators and provide business support to start-ups. It organises conferences, seminars, annual entrepreneur awards and dissemination activities, providing entrepreneurship training courses and consultancy, and facilitating access to financing and technology/knowledge transfer. It is meant to propose legislation and to develop proposals of incentives for entrepreneurs. In addition to this, it fosters co-operation with educational institutions and other relevant agencies to promote a culture of leadership and personal initiative, and facilitates networks between academia and the business community to promote the transfer of knowledge and technology.[3]

In 2014, the SME Policy Unit was created in the Ministry of Economy to carry out policy evaluation, monitoring and foster and international relations. The unit should also conduct policy advocacy and national policy co-ordination. It should be headed by the chairperson of Libya Enterprise and supervised by the SME Steering Committee. Due to the political instability in the country, the unit has been delayed in advancing its work on SME policy issues.

Five regional SME funds were created to deal with regional disparities and provide financing for SME projects in their respective regions, but they are not yet operational. The institutions responsible for managing the regional funds are supposed to provide a range of SME support functions, but they will require substantial institutional capacities and well-functioning checks and balances that will take time and political commitment to build.

Establishing a dedicated agency for delivery of SME policy and programmes is consistent with international good practices (OECD/UNIDO, 2004). Libya Enterprise – or a similar national SME agency – should therefore remain in place, and its authority should be strengthened. There is some speculation that the government may disband Libya Enterprise and devolve its activities into the five regional SME funds. Setting up the regional funds is a positive step in terms of accommodating and responding to regional differences in entrepreneurship and SME development. But there is still a need for a national co-ordination mechanism working in concert with the regional funds. This must be considered further in order to clarify the structure for implementing the national SME strategy.

Co-ordination mechanisms

Libya's institutional framework was already considered very complex and opaque before 2011 (Transtec, 2010), but it has gotten worse over the past years. Because SME development is a horizontal policy issue, and policies affecting SMEs concern a number of ministries and government agencies, co-ordination mechanisms are very important. Without it, there is a great risk of fragmentation, overlap and duplication.

The Ministry of Economy, under oversight of the SME Steering Committee, should be responsible for SME policy co-ordination within the government. Given the mandate of the steering committee is limited to addressing the co-ordination issues for a wide-reaching SME strategy, the Ministry of Economy recommended to the ministers' council that a more encompassing inter-ministerial body be established. This council would report to the prime minister on all activities, strategies, funds and institutions that support SMEs in all sectors and would supervise the regional funds and technical assistance activities. The formation of such an inter-ministerial committee would be consistent with international good practice in SME policy structures (OECD/UNIDO, 2004). When formed, such a council should be accountable for approval of the proposed national SME strategy and monitoring its implementation against performance targets and benchmarks. An additional co-ordination mechanism could be set up to deal with broader competitiveness reforms on issues that affect SMEs and development of the private sector, such as the investment climate, business environment, financial sector reforms and competition reforms.

Public-private consultation mechanisms

There are currently no institutionalised mechanisms for policy dialogue between the government, business associations and civil society organisations (CSOs). This is partly due to the lack of SME-related non-governmental and private sector associations, which were forbidden for a long time. The main business organisations are the chambers of commerce and the Libyan Business Council (LBC). The national Union of the Chambers of Commerce combines the 14 chambers across Libya and reports to the Ministry of Economy. Since the Ministry of Economy appoints a third of the members of the board of directors of the chambers, they are not independent. By law, it is compulsory for all businesses and persons engaged in commercial/industrial/service activity to register with the chambers. However, commercial chambers lack formal platforms to voice their concerns to the government (Hachmeier, 2013). The LBC, formed in 2011 to contribute to the reconstruction of Libyan business in co-ordination with the Libyan National Council, participates in the preparation and formulation of economic legislation and provides opinions to the competent authorities. It also develops proposals to enable businesses to carry out of their duties properly and encourage the establishment and expansion of the Islamic banking system and financial institutions. Although the LBC does engage in dialogue with Libya Enterprise, its institutional capacity is limited.

The Department for International Development (DfID) initiated a project, "Strengthening Libyan Private Sector Development Institutions/LPSDI" (2013-16), to build the capacity of Libyan business associations to provide more services to SMEs (DfID, 2013). But more is needed to encourage the formation of representative business associations and build their capacity to perform a policy advocacy function.

The Ministry of Economy or Libya Enterprise should create a more formal consultation mechanism for gathering the views of business associations and chambers of commerce on SME policy needs. A common choice of governments in a number of countries is to create an advisory committee on SMEs and entrepreneurship, with a mandate to represent the views of the SME sector and provide policy advice to the government, including input on the potential impact of proposed legislation on SMEs. Such committees are comprised of representatives from the key business/SME associations, a number of entrepreneurs and SME owners, experts in SME development and possibly service providers.

4.2. SME policy measures

During the past ten years, consecutive governments in Libya introduced policy measures to support SMEs. These include financial assistance programmes, programmes to support start-ups and create a more entrepreneurial culture and initiatives to improve access to entrepreneurship training, information and advice. More could be done to diversify the sources and types of financing, broaden the reach and scope of enterprise support services and improve their effectiveness, strengthen the capacity of existing SMEs, improve their market access and encourage innovation activity.

4.2.1. SME financing programmes

Access to finance continues to be the one of the top constraints for private enterprises in Libya, but there are few programmes supporting SME lending. Private investment is largely funded by personal equity (e.g. entrepreneurs' savings, loans from family and friends) and the level of bank financing to SMEs is very low. Commercial banks concentrate on heavily secured, short-term financing, such as export credits, and tend to favour established, large firms, rather than SMEs. Prior to the revolution, banks were criticised for failing to back private-sector enterprises, especially the riskier SME sector, however, they defended their position by stating that the legal framework of the Gaddafi era did not offer sufficient protection for their loans. There are no regulatory policies to encourage banks to engage in lending to SMEs except for the state-guaranteed lending fund. On the other hand, some banks have independently established SME windows.[4]

Credit guarantee scheme

Globally, credit guarantee mechanisms are one of the most widespread ways of defraying inordinate risk connected with debt financing from banks, particularly for new projects. Guarantee funds of up to 70%+ are used to underwrite part of the loan issued by a commercial bank, depending on the country, which reduces the risk to the commercial bank and, in well-functioning markets, promotes easier and less costly access to credit for SMEs. Credit guarantee programmes also help banks gain experience in dealing with SMEs and assess the financing risk of their loan requests. They typically target SMEs and start-ups constrained in their access to credit because of under-collateralisation and lack of credit histories, track records in business and capacity to develop bankable proposals.

The government established the Libyan Guarantee Lending Fund in 2008 under the supervision of the Ministry of Economy and support from Libya Enterprise. This fund draws up agreements with individual commercial banks to lend to SMEs on a guaranteed basis according to enterprise and loan size criteria set by Libya Enterprise.[5] The fund is not fully functioning and needs reactivation. Anecdotal evidence suggests that default rates are high, and many of the projects supported are in sectors not likely to make a substantial contribution to long-term development goals (e.g. construction and retail). Not only does the process of reimbursing commercial banks in case of default takes six to seven years, the scheme does not cover all banks, and the fund is not an independent entity (OECD/EC/ETF, 2014). Thus, the scheme is not achieving significant results in channelling bank financing to meet the needs of SMEs.

International experience shows that the design of credit guarantee schemes is critical. Objectives, target population, coverage ratio, cost structure and credit risk evaluation should ensure additionality by supporting access to finance for SMEs, while at the same time not subsidising undue risk-taking or crowding-out of commercial finance (OECD, 2013). Many countries, including in the MENA region, have achieved considerable success in channelling bank financing to SMEs by setting up a formal credit guarantee agency, something Libya could consider. Good practice models in the MENA region from which Libya can learn are illustrated by the *Caisse Centrale de Garantie* in Morocco and *Kafalat* in Lebanon (see good practice profiles in AfDB, 2015: 48-70). These examples also point to the importance of developing a range of guarantee products to respond to the short- and medium-term financing needs of start-ups and SMEs at different stages of development or meet economy development objectives (e.g. for innovative projects and export activity), including sectoral priorities.

Microfinance industry

Microfinance can fill the gap for unbankable start-ups and micro and small enterprises, particularly from vulnerable groups, such as youth and women. In most developing countries, including in the MENA region, microfinance is provided by non-governmental organisations (NGOs), which for many decades were not permitted to form in Libya. In a number of MENA countries, the microfinance industry is well developed, for example, Morocco and Egypt. To develop the industry, governments in these countries have developed regulatory frameworks for microfinance institutions and instituted codes of good practice. Although the Rural Bank appears to play a role in providing micro-enterprise financing in rural areas, there is no regulatory framework for microfinance. On an ad hoc basis, the Islamic Development Bank (IsDB) and the Libyan Ministry of Economy have launched a USD 50 million project to offer Islamic microfinance services to unemployed Libyan youth in line with the IsDB's Arab Youth Employment Support Programme, but much more should be done to broaden access to microfinance services for productive projects.

Concessional financing

Concessional financing from government funds or development banks has been one of the major forms of financing available to stimulate private investment and diversify Libya's economy away from oil. They sometimes targeted SMEs, for example, the EUR 188 million

Libyan Loan Fund created in 2010 under the supervision of the National Council for Economic and Social Development.[6] There is no accessible data on how much concessional debt has been issued since 2011. However, the overall non-performing loan ratio in the economy is close to 30%, indicating the government of Libya has not made a serious effort to ensure repayment. Also, the lack of commercial financing of Libyan investment could be at least partially traced to crowding-out by concessional mechanisms.

Two major state-owned investment entities, the Economic and Social Development Fund (ESDF) and the Libyan Local Investment and Development Fund (LLIDF), were created to boost the role of the private sector in economic growth, diversify the non-oil economy and improve the environment for investors across Libya.[7] These funds favour private investment in large development projects, often through use of public-private partnerships (PPPs) that will bring in foreign expertise and technology, and are not so available for SMEs. The funds also have weak governance structures and lack transparent and clear legal and regulatory frameworks and co-ordination. There is evidence that the ESDF may have destabilised the banking sector through politically motivated, ad hoc investment programmes and crowded-out credit to the non-ESDF private sector. The LLIDF may have further undermined market forces and limited private sector development (World Bank, 2013).

Given the demand from companies for concessional equity mechanisms and the strong need for diversification and investment into new insufficiently explored sectors, this mechanism is likely to continue to play a strong role, especially given the difficulties in securing financing from commercial banks. However, such funds should be institutionally independent, target investment with a clear strategic value to the medium- and long-term economic development of the country and apply commercial criteria wherever possible. Allowing outside investors to participate in the capital of the funds is one mechanism to make sure investment decisions are sufficiently vetted and monitored.

Regional SME funds

In 2013, the government established five regional investment funds in Tripoli, Benghazi, Misrata, Dernia and Sebha to support start-ups and new SME projects. Capitalised with LYD 200 million each (about USD 150 million) for a total of LYD 1 billion, the funds were meant to provide financing by participating with equity of up to 25% of project capital, co-financing and guaranteeing the bank portion of the loan. The agreement with local banks allows for credit of up to 40% of the project cost, provided the SME investors participate with some of their own capital (5%–10%, depending on the size of the project). The size of loans is determined by the scale of the SME: loans of LYD 1 000-100 000 for micro-enterprises; up to LYD 1 million for small enterprises; and LYD 1 million-5 million for medium enterprises, with the business co-funding at least 10% of the project costs. Particularly through the guarantee mechanism and the equity participation, the funds are intended to leverage a considerable amount of bank financing to the SME sector. They shoul also provide training, consultancy and monitoring of all approved projects through Libya Enterprise, which, if properly delivered, should have a positive impact on the success of the projects. The funds are not yet all operational and are subject to the allocation of financing by the Ministry of Planning, which has been paralysed by the political and fiscal situation.

Although these funds could have a positive impact, it is unclear whether an additional concessional capital provision will address the underlying problems facing the Libyan economy, in particular fixing financial intermediation. Unless rigorously structured, the funds risk exacerbating problems, such as the crowding-out of commercial finance and the already high levels of non-performing loans (NPLs).

Private venture capital industry

There are no private equity or venture capital funds in Libya. Over the years, in the absence of private equity funds, the Libyan government has established publicly-owned funds to support Libya's economic diversification and private sector development (e.g. EDSF and LIIDF), but these have not targeted SMEs.

In the medium term, as the private sector expands, the demand for venture capital could be expected to grow. At the same time, international experience shows that public policy actions are often necessary to stimulate the supply of private venture capital funds, such as through providing tax incentives, offering matching funding or establishing government funds managed by private fund managers, and inviting other investors to partner in the funds. All of these policy measures seek to reduce the risk for private investors and increase their potential return, making it more attractive for them to invest in promising and innovative start-ups and early-stage ventures. International experience also shows that as a private venture capital industry evolves over time – which could take as much as ten years – the government can withdraw as a direct equity investor, except in cases where it might seek to address persistent market failures, such as for equity investments in high-risk, innovative start-ups and promising early-stage companies.

The national SME strategy should include policy measures to develop a private venture capital industry in Libya, which may be able to attract capital investment from international financial organisations, such as the European Bank for Reconstruction and Development (EBRD) and IsBD, which have been helping to capitalise venture funds in other MENA countries.

4.2.2. Entrepreneurship development and start-up support

The main instruments for providing entrepreneurship and start-up support are the Libya Enterprise Centres (LECs) and business incubators, both under Libya Enterprise and the business centres operated by the LPRD for former combatants.

Libya Enterprise Centres

Libya Enterprise Starting created a network of 13 LECs. Almost all LECs are located in the northeast and northwest regions along the Mediterranean coast, with three in the interior and southern regions (Sebha, Gherian and Alzintan). These include the Tripoli Women's Enterprise Centre (WEC) and the Enterprise Centre for Disabled Persons. In 2014, more than half of these centres were still under construction, and the activities of operational centres were curtailed because of the conflict.

These centres provide short training courses that help entrepreneurs develop their business ideas, undertake a feasibility study and learn about project management and the logistics of starting a business. They also offer some consultation services to prepare feasibility studies and guidance on developing business plans. Of the 3 750 entrepreneurs trained to the end of 2014, only 650 feasibility studies had been prepared and 317 projects approved for the guaranteed lending fund.[8] This indicates some inefficiencies in the programme structure or delivery that need to be addressed, as it would not be unusual to have a start-up rate of 30% among trainees in an entrepreneurship training programme. In 2015, the Libya Enterprise budget proposal for the centres projected to train 1 350 entrepreneurs in 160 training courses, prepare 575 feasibility studies (50% for micro projects, 35% for small projects and 15% for medium projects) and nurture 16 pilot projects for entrepreneurs with innovative ideas (Libya Enterprise, 2015).

However, the LECs do not offer a broad range of responsive business development support (BDS) services dealing with the operational aspects of business management. Nor do they provide mentoring and coaching support, which are normally provided by such centres in other countries. The support seems to stop after the feasibility study and business plan stages. Follow-up services are not provided to help entrepreneurs through the start-up and early-stage development of their businesses. As well, services are not generally offered to existing SMEs.

Metrics for the LECs are not available, but Libya Enterprise should be collecting data from the centres on a regular basis. Libya Enterprise reports that some LECs perform better than others in terms of entrepreneurs completing the training, the number of quality of businesses started and jobs created. More consistent performance results might be achieved by aligning institutional incentives with a more stringent screening process for accepting applicants into the entrepreneurship training, including an assessment of their commitment to the programme. Budget allocation to the centres could be a function of the success rate in converting the trainees into start-ups.[9]

A baseline survey was conducted in 2013 of 314 SMEs. Only 2% had received training, technical support, incubation or other services from Libya Enterprise, and the training was often perceived to be of little value (Upper Quartile, 2013a). This suggests that improvements in the quality, and perhaps duration, of the training programmes are necessary. The outcomes from entrepreneurship training may also be improved by implementing standardised and internationally-proven training materials and approaches to raise the quality and consistency of the training. Many developing countries have achieved impressive results by utilising programmes, such as the "Start Your Business" (SYB),[10] developed and promoted by the International Labour Organization (ILO) and already translated into Arabic for use in Egypt, Jordan and Morocco, or EMPRETEC courses, sponsored by the United Nations Conference on Trade and Development (UNCTAD).[11] Adopting these programmes would require partnerships with sponsoring organisations, training of certified Libyan trainers to deliver the programmes and making the training workshops available to Libyans throughout the country. These or similar entrepreneurship training programmes would impart entrepreneurial competencies to aspiring entrepreneurs, bring them closer to starting a business and improve their chances of success once started.

The WEC was established in Tripoli to promote entrepreneurship among women, but it is not clear whether it is currently functional. Establishing women's entrepreneurship centres can be an effective approach to helping women start and develop their own businesses (OECD, 2012b). It works both with aspiring women entrepreneurs – including female graduates of universities and institutes – and existing women entrepreneurs who want to expand their businesses through offers of entrepreneurship training programmes, technical support and specialised consultancy based on the specific challenges faced by the women. It also provides a follow-up after the launch of the projects through field visits to advise the women entrepreneurs on how to overcome any difficulties that might be impeding their success, including guidance on promotion and marketing.

The Voice of Libyan Women (VLW), an NGO founded in 2011, recommended that the government establish a network of women's enterprise centres around the country to counsel women entrepreneurs and provide training, mentorship and networking opportunities to help them start and grow businesses (VLW, 2012). This should also include organising regional and national women entrepreneur forums to facilitate dialogue on how the government can expand support to women-owned businesses.

LPRD business centres for ex-combatants

Ex-combatants are an important target group for entrepreneurship training and support in Libya because of their number. As many as 240 000 ex-combatants are looking for work, but opportunities to integrate them into the workforce are limited (DfID, 2013). The LPRD's Tumuh SME Project aims to provide entrepreneurship training to 70 000 former combatants and create 7 000 new businesses over a four-year period that will help grow the private sector, diversify the economy, and create jobs. The LPRD has trained 80 business consultants to work with ex-combatants in several regions of Libya and initiated four business centres. More are planned to host the business consultants and provide services to the ex-combatants. In addition, contracted local and international experts will conduct a nationwide economic map and feasibility study to determine the best sort of entrepreneurial projects in each region (LPRD, 2015). Between 2012 and 2014, expenditure on the Tumuh SME Project was LYD 8.75 million, about 12.5% of the LPRD's total direct spending. The average funding per project is LYD 100 000. This project has great potential to develop private enterprises and create value in Libyan society and should be monitored carefully for impact and success.

Libya Enterprise business incubators

The Business Incubators Programme was launched in March 2009 to promote new start-ups, diversify the economy and reduce youth unemployment. The primary targets of the incubator are new graduates, unemployed youth and women. LYD 20 billion was to be allocated to the programme for the launch of five business incubators. Libya Enterprise currently operates a network of six business incubators: three general business incubators based in Tripoli, Benghazi and Sebha; two specialised business incubators (the Agricultural Technology Incubator in Tripoli and the Bani Walid Information and Communications Technology [ICT] incubator); and Benghazi University Incubator. Two more were under construction in 2015.

However, Libyan stakeholders indicate that incubator programmes are either delayed or only partially implemented because of budget constraints. Anecdotal evidence suggests low activity levels and few projects that could be considered innovative. Currently, the Libyan incubators provide three services: free work stations, free internet access and technical support to help the entrepreneurs develop feasibility studies and business plans.

Incubators in developed countries commonly offer entrepreneurship training, management development workshops and seminars, mentoring from experienced business advisors and entrepreneurs, linkages to other support agencies for specialised technical assistance and opportunities for the entrepreneurs to pitch their business proposals to investor networks or other sources of seed capital/financing (Box 4.1). In some cases, the incubator itself manages a seed capital fund. The DfID started a project in 2013 to support the Libya Enterprise incubators by building the capacity of staff and services, preparing a business plan with funding and staffing requirements and providing technical assistance to help the incubators in designing a suite of SME support services (DfID, 2013). In the long term, Libya Enterprise should expand the network of incubators to more parts of the country.

The Ministry of Economy and Libya Enterprise should develop a data system to systematically collect information from the incubators on: the number of incubator applicants, the acceptance rate of new projects, the incubation time required for each enterprise, the jobs created during the incubation process, the number of enterprises graduating from the incubator, the revenue and employment figures at the time of graduation, the graduate firm survival rates over time and growth in the number of jobs created by graduate firms and their revenues. These metrics will enable the government to measure the effectiveness of the incubator programme, as well as the comparative performance of the individual incubators and the value for money spent.

Libya Enterprise could consider setting up clear criteria for project selection and making sure that projects are innovative. Forging stronger university linkages may help in finding potential entrepreneurs among university students and faculty and transferring and adapting foreign technologies to Libyan start-ups.

Libya Enterprise could also explore the model of business accelerators, which focus on fast-tracking start-ups through three- to six-month programmes of idea development and pre-incubation for entrepreneurs with high-potential business ideas and rapid growth ambitions. This is common in other countries, including in the MENA region.[12]

Box 4.1. **Good practice in management of national incubation systems**

Successful business incubation systems develop national operating guidelines or standards for the operation of individual facilities. Developing governance and performance standards, as well as designing monitoring and appraisal mechanisms, can improve the performance of business incubators (infoDev, 2010). This includes the following:

- developing a manual of operating guidelines and performance standards for the range of services provided, which cover: helping with preparing feasibility studies and business plans; coaching and mentoring for new entrepreneurs by experienced entrepreneurs and experts; basic legal advisory services; assistance with product development, intellectual property issues and marketing; and providing links to sources of financing and investment capital
- preparing a standard list of qualifications and experience for recruitment processes to facilitate the selection of effective, committed and knowledgeable management and staff
- implementing professional development programmes to build the capacity of incubator managers, staff and advisors to provide the highest level of support to incubating start-ups.

Complementary start-up and entrepreneurship support programmes and initiatives

International organisations are also supporting entrepreneurship initiatives in Libya. With DfID funding, Dutch NGO SPARK launched the Benghazi Entrepreneurship Centre (BEC) in 2013 to support young aspiring entrepreneurs and SMEs and raise awareness of entrepreneurship among youth.[13] The centre uses SPARK's standardised business skills and training modules and works with local business experts to train and coach the beneficiaries. It offers start-up training and a business accelerator programme to university students, recent graduates, aspiring women entrepreneurs and ex-combatants in the 18-35 age group. BEC hosts business plan competitions, providing training and coaching to support the best business ideas and helping entrepreneurs start their businesses. In some cases, the business plan competitions are targeted to expansion plans of existing SMEs. It works in close co-operation with the University of Benghazi Research and Consulting Centre, Libyan banks and potential investors to support its start-up entrepreneurs.

In 2013, the United States Agency for International Development (USAID), in partnership with the Mennonite Economic Development Associates (MEDA) and the Libya Women's Forum, launched the USD 1.14 million Libya Women's Economic Empowerment (LWEE) project to enhance women's entrepreneurship development in Libya. The objectives of the project are to give Libyan businesswomen the chance to grow during Libya's transition period, help create a more diversified economy and build a vibrant private sector. Training, coaching/mentorship, networking and buyer engagement is provided to women owners of mid-level SMEs to enable the development and expansion of their businesses. The project includes a business plan competition for women entrepreneurs, supported by personalised training and mentoring to refine their business strategies, and access to a matching grant ranging from LYD 5 000 to LYD 30 000 to provide the seed capital needed to advance their businesses to the next level. The project is also building the capacity of local partners to provide services to women business owners and assisting in the creation of a network of Libyan women entrepreneurs. The project, extended to 2016, has a target to provide technical support to 210 women entrepreneurs and create 700 new jobs.[14]

Demand for the LWEE programme has been high, demonstrating great interest from women entrepreneurs to improve their performance. By mid-2015, the LWEE project had processed 13 training groups and trained over 200 entrepreneurial women from Tripoli, Benghazi and Zawia on fundamental business skills, including finance, administration and management, marketing and leadership. Consideration should be given to scaling up and funding this programme on an ongoing basis to raise the capacity and economic contribution of women-owned SMEs in Libya.

4.2.3. Capacity building of existing SMEs

There appears to be insufficient business support for existing SMEs in Libya. They are not generally the target of Libya Enterprise programmes and no alternative support structures exist to help them overcome developmental obstacles or improve their performance. The EU/Expertise France-funded project, "Support to Libya for Economic Integration, Diversification and Sustainable Employment", started in 2014, may be helpful in filling this gap. The project aims to set up ten micro, small and medium enterprise (MSME) support centres in various sites throughout Libya in partnership with relevant local institutions (e.g. local councils, local chambers of commerce and industry, universities, CSOs) (Expertise France, 2014). These centres are to have the capacity to provide mentoring, advisory support and consultancy services to entrepreneurs planning to start a business or expand their operations. Presumably, they will be more in line with international good practices in providing BDS services and doing so in areas of the country not covered by existing LECs.

The project involves setting up a national co-ordination structure for the MSME support centres, also an important component. This co-ordination structure will develop and mobilise national consultancy capacity, prepare advisory materials and facilitate local access to appropriate technical and advisory services, which should lead to improved competencies of advisors and consultants, better quality services, and improved access of services to entrepreneurs in more regions of the country.

The chambers of commerce can also provide business support for existing SMEs. Most SMEs know their local chambers and have registered with them. However, the chambers have a very low capacity to deliver services to the business community (Upper Quartile, 2013b) and cater more to issues of the medium and large businesses (GIZ, 2013). Relatively few SMEs make use of chamber services but appreciate support in obtaining a business license, facilitation of their import and export activities, legal advice and networking services with Libyan and foreign companies and investors. According to the Upper Quartile (2013a) baseline survey of MSMEs, only 5% of the MSMEs registered with the chamber were satisfied with the services provided by their local chamber and found them useful. The Libyan Private Sector Development Institutions (LPSDI) project seeks to build capacity of the chambers so they can become more proactive business support organisations, which provide business advisory services and help member businesses grow and create employment for more Libyans (DfID, 2013).

Another approach adopted by many countries, sometimes in partnership with chambers of commerce, is to develop dedicated programmes to upgrade the capacity of existing SMEs so as to raise their level of productivity and competitiveness. Usually the first step is to undertake a diagnosis to identify the core productivity challenges and develop an action plan to remedy deficiencies and support access to financing the SMEs' costs

Box 4.2. Algeria's SME upgrading programme

The *Mise à Niveau* SME upgrading programme, implemented by the National Agency for the Development of SMEs (ANDPME), addresses the challenge of improving the competitiveness of the national economy in general and business in particular. The approach aims to intensify and diversify the economic base, improve the competitiveness of companies across multiple areas and strengthen their position in the marketplace. The programme supports a process of continuous learning to influence new attitudes and behaviour of entrepreneurs and encourage the adoption of more innovative management approaches and systems. The upgrading process goes through several stages tailored to the needs of each participating enterprise.

Phase 1: The preparatory step raises the entrepreneur's awareness of his/her shortcomings and those of the company. It involves a process of diagnosis which allows identification and validation of the main business problems. Up to 80% of the consultancy costs are covered by the programme, with a maximum of DZD 400 000 (about USD 5 000) for pre-diagnosis services, and up to DZD 2 million (about USD 25 000) for diagnostic services. The SME covers the remaining costs.

Phase 2: Consultants work with the company on the adoption of good management practices, establishing a more functional organisation and optimising business functions. The programme subsidises between 10% and 80% of the costs incurred to hire consultants and invest in equipment, technology and information systems. The percentage depends on the size of the SME's turnover and whether the costs are for consultants or investments in technology or other physical upgrades.

Phase 3: The company addresses the issues identified. Upgrading actions include: strengthening human resources at various levels; learning to delegate responsibilities to teams and trust workers' skills; gaining a better understanding of SME markets and positioning; and implementing management methods according to the sector and the specific needs of the enterprise (e.g. inventory management, project management, production management, etc.). The programme subsidises up to 80% of the cost of management training (up to DZD 400 000) and specialised coaching in exporting, innovation, financial management and certification (up to DZD 800 000). If the SME seeks certification, the programme will subsidise only 20% of the costs (up to DZD 1 million, about USD 12 500).

Phase 4: The entrepreneur starts anticipating and planning for the future development of the company through actions such as complying with international standards and determining new product and market strategies.

Source: Programme National de Mise à Niveau des PME (National SME Upgrading Programme), National Agency for SME Development, Algeria, www.andpme.org.dz/index.php/fr/mise-a-niveau-3/.

of implementing recommendations. This financial assistance can be applied to costs incurred to acquire new technology to improve production processes and information systems, pursue ISO9000 certification, upgrade the skills of workers, etc. (Box 4.2). The national SME strategy should include an SME upgrading component to address the low productivity and competitiveness of Libyan SMEs and improve their ability to compete in domestic and international markets.

4.2.4. Access to domestic markets: procurement policies and supply chain linkages

Libyan authorities could develop policy initiatives to improve domestic market access for SMEs, as is commonly the case in other countries, specifically SME-friendly public procurement policies and supply chain linkages.

SME-friendly public procurement policies

The process of bidding and awarding public procurement contracts in Libya is heavily discretionary. Principles of fair competition are not applied between domestic and foreign firms. For example, in 2010 Libyan firms were only allowed to bid for procurement contracts with a maximum level of 20 times their capital, while tenders were open for foreign firms (Transtec, 2010). In terms of legal framework, the last public procurement regulation was issued in 2007. In 2012, the Ministry of Planning acknowledged the need to eliminate corruption, inefficiencies and unclear procedures and implement international standards for public contracting, such as those consistent with the recognised principles and instruments of the 2015 OECD Recommendation on Public Procurement.[15] However, there has not been much progress due to political instability.

Given the large scale of public sector and SOE purchasing, public procurement presents a significant opportunity to expand the market potential for domestic SMEs. Generally speaking, it is harder for SMEs than for large businesses to participate in public procurement processes. They face higher pre-qualification, qualification, bid and proposal costs, not to mention others associated with accessing information about the bidding process. They also face formidable burdens in obtaining bid and performance bonds and guarantees, which can be a significant factor in their ability to compete for procurement tenders. In addition, SMEs often lack the working capital resources to wait for payment, which tends to take very long. Governments and contracting authorities at the central and local level in many countries seek to actively improve levels of SME participation in public sector contracts by implementing policies and measures to reduce the transaction costs and alleviate the information problems that SMEs face in the public procurement process. The rationale for such policies is to enable SMEs to compete more effectively for public contracts. By creating domestic markets for SMEs, SME-friendly procurement policies can lead to both enterprise and employment growth. It is important to develop a public procurement strategy policy for SMEs, with preferably a mandatory use by public entities. Moreover, the results should be measured in order to assess the policy impact.

Some countries set regulatory targets for the minimum percentage of public procurement contracts (i.e. a value) to be awarded to SMEs. For example, the US Small Business Administration has a minimum set-aside of 23% of all federal contracts for small businesses.[16] A number of countries in the MENA region have now also adopted regulations and policies for awarding procurement contracts to SMEs (Box 4.3). In Serbia, the Administration for Joint Services, which is responsible for centralised public procurement, is obliged to cut tenders into lots whenever possible. Moreover, the legislation also enables contracting authorities to require those tendering for contracts above certain thresholds to subcontract part of the contract to SMEs. Set-asides and quotas have to be complemented by further simplification of tender requirements and submission processes. Simplification measures can include:

- simplifying the tendering documents and procedures
- having in place a sound and efficient E-procurement system which fosters transparency, access to information (including access to procurement opportunities and tender documents), and decreases the administrative costs of suppliers (i.e. travel, copies/ printing, postage costs)
- de-bundling large contract tenders with a technical or regional allotment strategy
- implementing a SME-supplier registration system (with an easy process to register) that allows them to be pre-qualified as bidders
- relieving the financial capacity requirements
- limiting the requirements in terms of bid bonds and performance of bonds, and simplifying the process to get them from the financial institutions
- allowing for suppliers grouping (consortium) and sub-contracting
- improving transparency and ensuring objectivity in the process by eliminating opportunities for corruption and bribery in the allocation of final awards would also be necessary to increase the access of SMEs to public procurement
- providing information and training to SMEs on how to successfully access procurement contracts
- making available tender documents for free.

Box 4.3. SME-related public procurement policies in selected MENA countries

Morocco: The Moroccan Decree No. 2-12-349 issued in 2013, allocates 20% of the total value of public procurement contracts to SMEs. To realise this target, the government will have to develop a system for determining how much procurement is currently awarded to SMEs and implement a tracking system to monitor the volume of procurement awards going to SMEs. It will also have to make specific efforts to provide information to SMEs on procurement processes and how to prepare tender proposals, and implement business support initiatives to help SMEs upgrade the quality of their products to meet the standards of procurement specifications. Moreover, in case of sub-contracting, the decree gives the possibility to public officials to impose in the tender documents suppliers to have local or SME sub-contractors.

Tunisia: The government regulated allocation of public procurement contracts to SMEs in the 2014 Decree on Public Procurement (Decree No. 1039), allocating 20% of the total contract value to SMEs. However, participation of SMEs had reached only 7% of the value of procurement contracts. In 2011, it issued further regulations to facilitate their participation in tenders by providing SMEs with favourable financial conditions, such as exemption from the mandatory advance of 20% of the contract and the provisional bonds required within the first five years of establishment (Decree no. 2011-623).

Box 4.3. SME-related public procurement policies in selected MENA countries *(continued)*

Egypt: The 2004 Egyptian Small Enterprise Development Law (Law 141/2004) allocates 10% of government contracts to enterprises with fewer than 50 employees (micro and small enterprises). An inter-ministerial committee on SME procurement was formed under the Ministry of Finance in 2004 to determine the policies and measures required to meet this quota. The Government Authority of Government Services (GAGS) analysed the procurement categories that would be most conducive to SME bidders, implemented a process of breaking large procurement contracts into smaller lots, carried out an awareness campaign to educate SMEs about the procurement process and opportunities, and provided training to procurement officers from different ministries and departments on SME-sensitive practices.

United Arab Emirates: Under the SME Law (Federal Law No. 2 of 2014) federal authorities and ministries must contract at least 10% of their procurement budget for purchasing, servicing and consulting to SMEs. Government-related firms, in which the federal government holds stakes of more than 25%, must also ensure at least 5% of their contracts are with SMEs.

Linking SMEs to markets through supply chain programmes

SMEs are often thwarted in their efforts to break into supply chains of large domestic and multinational enterprises because they lack the capacity and ability to meet performance and quality standards. Supplier development and supply-chain linkage programmes are an effective way to improve the capability of SMEs to act as suppliers to large firms. They are important in two ways. First, they can upgrade the ability of SMEs to act as sub-contractors and suppliers to large enterprises, which increases their market potential and raises their ultimate capacity to engage in exporting activity. Second, having a supply of qualified domestic SME suppliers in a country is an important attraction factor for FDI. Global value chains (GVCs) are likely to grow in importance, and governments seeking to increase the role played by SMEs should raise awareness of supply chain opportunities among SMEs, foster linkages between SMEs and large firms and support them in the process of complying with international standards (OECD, 2008).

There is no evidence of concerted efforts of the Libyan government to develop supply chain linkages between SMEs and large firms, including SOEs and foreign firms. According to the 2014-2015 Global Competitiveness Index (GCI), the quantity of local suppliers is moderate, with the country ranking 58 out of 144 countries. But the quality and production process sophistication of these suppliers is low, with a rank of 142. The state of cluster development and the value chain breadth are also low: the ranks for these two factors are 140 and 143 respectively (Schwab, 2014).

In 2012, the government developed a "Near Term Plan for SME Development in Libya" in co-operation with the Deauville Partnership. It committed under this plan to expand the capacity of SMEs to integrate in GVCs (OECD, 2012a). This included the following points:

- developing programmes to coach SME managers in areas such as design and production engineering and providing technical advice on upgrading of production processes and quality standards
- co-opting agreements with foreign companies and SOEs to participate in formal supplier development programmes to upgrade small groups of SME suppliers to meet their standards is a critical component.

- establishing a programme to raise awareness of opportunities for participating in global value chains by providing information on market opportunities for subcontracting purposes, reports and data bases, trade fairs, exhibitions abroad and electronic trading platforms
- promoting the development of clusters and networks for SMEs and strengthening links with universities, research institutions and other SMEs
- identifying a few pilot value chains, notably in construction materials and food processing, and funding pilot co-operation projects between SMEs and foreign firms.

Supply chain development should be considered one of the priorities in the national SME strategy, and action encompassing the above points should be taken (Box 4.4).

Box 4.4. Policy options in trade for GVC integration by SMEs in low-income developing countries

Firms in low-income developing countries (LIDCs) face significant challenges to accessing GVCs, including a less supportive domestic operating environment and weaker institutions. This leads to higher fixed costs and challenges to compete in international markets. As a result, LIDCs are under-represented in GVCs.

SMEs in LIDCs predominantly operate in the informal economy, and their participation in GVCs is concentrated in the agricultural sector and labor-intensive, very low value-added manufacturing and services activities, where entry costs are lower and not capital intensive. At the same time, most SMEs in developed economies participate in GVCs mainly as domestic suppliers of exporters, much more than through direct exports only. Policy action can make a difference in achieving more inclusive GVCs, but it requires a holistic approach to reform, spanning trade, investment and domestic policies. This includes the following:

- addressing human capital deficiencies through policies that combine high-quality initial education with lifelong learning opportunities for all to help ensure workers are well prepared for the future
- supporting innovation through product innovation, process and organisational change and adoption of ICT technology
- reducing trade costs through trade facilitation and logistics, import tariff streamlining, simplification of export procedures and provision of targeted services
- supporting SMEs meeting certification and quality standards
- developing innovative financial instruments to allow young and innovative SMEs and firms to participate in GVCs, with a particular focus on equity financing
- developing statistical capacity to identify the main bottlenecks and set policy priorities.

Source: OECD and World Bank Group, *Inclusive Value Chains,* report prepared for submissions to G20 Trade Ministers Meeting, Istanbul, October 2015.

4.2.5. International market access: export development support

SMEs face many common challenges in developing their markets, particularly as trade agreements open up both domestic and export markets to increased competition and opportunities. Relatively high product cost structures, low product quality and limited marketing resources are frequently significant barriers for SMEs in accessing both domestic and export markets. Other challenges in accessing export markets are obtaining information on export markets, making contact with potential overseas customers, excessive transportation and insurance costs, lack of know-how regarding the steps to take and financing export activities.

Most governments aim to increase the percentage of exporting SMEs and to further internationalise their companies. Export market development priorities generally include increased awareness of the opportunities and challenges of exporting, improved information and intelligence, improved training, support and familiarisation systems and better export financing. Governments have also set up export support centres to provide information, counselling and access to government financial assistance programmes for SME exporters. Government-subsidised export market introduction or familiarisation programmes are common, as is the availability of specialised export financing institutions. Online tools are also widely used in developed countries to provide export information, intelligence and training.

Libya has undertaken several trade reforms in the last decade to liberalise the economy, and it has adhered to a number of regional trade agreements that could benefit the development of SMEs. However, there is no comprehensive export promotion strategy, and limited attempts have been made to assist SMEs in developing export markets. The Libyan Export Promotion Centre (LEPC) was established in 2006 as a semi-autonomous government-run organisation to promote exports, assist local companies in doing business abroad, serve as a focal point for co-ordination of export information with the private sector and train traders. Although it established a one-stop desk to deal with foreign trade procedures and offer trade-related services, trade facilitation processes remain relatively cumbersome, and no meaningful results have been achieved in diversifying from the hydrocarbon sectors. The LEPC developed an action plan in 2013 introducing new measures to encourage exports, such as direct subsidies to exporters, financial support for participation in national and international trade fairs and assistance in the design, production and marketing of exported goods, with a main focus on dates, olive oil, honey and fishery products (OECD/EC/ETF, 2014). In 2013, the government also established the Libya Trade Network to develop the movement of trade through the simplification of procedures and business dealings, including an e-system for foreign trade. But to date it has had minimal impact.

Libya's national SME strategy should include a policy component geared to enhancing opportunities for SMEs to engage in export activity, as well as helping SMEs overcome export barriers. This will require more proactive efforts to build the capacity of SMEs to pursue export markets. First, this should entail identifying the export potential of products and services and then developing an export marketing plan and making improvements in production processes and product quality to meet international standards. It will also require access to export financing. An appropriate option for Libya may be to support the development of SME export consortia, like Morocco did (Box 4.5).

In Libya, SME export consortia could be formed around opportunities in agri-foods, crafts, and other sectors where SME activity is dominant. The value of export consortia is that a group of SMEs are better able to achieve economies of scale in meeting the demands of export markets. SMEs are significantly present in the services sector in Libya but currently not very active in exporting these services.

Box 4.5. **Supporting SME exporters in Morocco**

In 2003, the Moroccan Ministry of Foreign Trade launched an export consortia support scheme to encourage the formation of export consortia among SMEs. Through the scheme, export consortia received co-funding of their promotional activities during the first three years of operation. MarocExport offered the consortia a preferential rate for participation at trade fairs and commercial missions compared to those offered to individual companies not in an export consortia. The Moroccan Export Insurance Company established a preferential premium for insurance policies issued to export consortia and offered them wide coverage for trade fair participation. The National Agency for Promotion of SMEs subsidised consulting costs for group-based modernisation and upgrading activities to meet international standards. By 2011, 21 export consortia had been legally formalised, covering 9 different sectors in 10 cities of the country, and involving 120 exporting SMEs employing 18 000 people.

In 2011, the Ministry of Foreign Trade, in co-operation with the Ministry of Economy and Finance and MarocExport, launched a follow-on "Export Synergia" Programme to stimulate the operation of 55 export consortia by 2015. Each new consortium, consisting of at least five SMEs with exporting capacity, is supported with up to MAD 1.5 million to cover the costs of forming the consortium, crafting a development strategy and undertaking international promotion and marketing activity.

Sources: Moroccan Ministry of Foreign Trade (www.mce.gov.ma/consortiums/presentation_nv_prog.pdf); "The UNIDO Export Consortia Programme Fact Sheet" (www.unido.org/fileadmin/import/82882_morocco_Factsheet.pdf).

4.2.6. Innovation and technological development support

Innovation ranges from simple incremental non-technological innovations in existing enterprises to radical technological innovations that have the potential to transform whole industries. Governments see particular value in supporting highly-innovative projects because of their wealth creation and high value-added job creation spillovers. Innovation in all aspects of a business, technological or otherwise, is a key factor in enhancing its productivity and competitiveness. SMEs need to increase innovation in the context of their product and service development and operational processes, as well as increasing their utilisation of ICTs and management information systems.

As countries make the transition from resource-based to knowledge-based economies, SME-related policy priorities become more focused on issues of modernisation, organisational linkages with research environments, the creation of innovation-supporting facilities, such as technology incubators, and the adoption of improved information technology (IT) systems. These include programmes or initiatives that provide funding assistance to aid SMEs in dealing with their R&D, technology development and commercialisation issues and encourage better integration of IT in operations.

Since developing technological ideas and turning them into commercially-viable ventures or projects is both costly and risky, governments are heavily involved in the financing of innovation-related activity through the use of R&D grants to cover the costs of prototype and proof-of-concept development, acquiring patents, researching market applications and related activities. They are also involved in incentive schemes to stimulate more private sector seed investment in innovative ventures in the early stages of commercialisation. Without this funding support, which may also take the form of tax incentives, many innovative SMEs and start-ups would not be able to garner the resources to advance their innovations to a market-ready state.

Several countries also capitalise on government-owned research institutions to assist and partner with SMEs in adopting and developing new technology. Developed countries, which have relatively strong public and private sector support structures for SMEs, are now targeting significant resources – including forms of risk capital – to advance the development of high-risk, enabling environmental, biotechnology and medical technologies. The trend is towards fostering dynamic innovation ecosystems that bring together a range of supports to spur the innovative and technological capacity of new start-ups and existing SMEs.

There is no evidence that Libyan policy is focused specifically on developing the potential for innovation of SMEs, although Libya Enterprise's work programme for 2015 had a goal to contribute to the transfer of knowledge, technology and support for local innovations through co-ordination with universities and research centres. It provides support related to intellectual property and domestic patents and has submitted a proposal for the establishment of a science park (Libya Enterprise, 2015). Some activities are taking place in the private sector. For example, the Libyan Business Council holds a competition for start-ups every year to promote innovative projects and ideas.

4.2.7. Promoting an entrepreneurial culture

Because of the importance of a vibrant entrepreneurial culture to increasing start-up and entrepreneurial activity rates, governments in many countries carry out wide-spread public campaigns to create awareness of entrepreneurship as a career/employment option and give more policy importance to entrepreneurship in the education system.

Given the weak entrepreneurship culture in Libya and low base of private sector activity, strong policy efforts are in this direction. This will require promoting an entrepreneurial culture through the media and the educational system, creating business opportunities and building the capacity of Libyans to identify and assess these opportunities from a market perspective.

Libya Enterprise organises an annual conference on entrepreneurship and innovation, an annual competition for entrepreneurship and innovation, an annual awards programme to recognise and celebrate entrepreneurial success and the Libya Global Entrepreneurship Week. In addition, the enterprise centres carry out activities to promote entrepreneurship in their local environments. Broader and wider-reaching promotional efforts that make use of mass media and roadshows in Libya's regions could also be considered in the future.

Educational institutions at all levels are important partners in entrepreneurship and SME development because of their role in producing a job-ready workforce with the knowledge and skills to meet the requirements of a modern market economy and its future entrepreneurs. Governments in many countries now consider entrepreneurship education as a policy objective of entrepreneurship and SME development strategies. Many initiatives have been implemented to promote the integration of entrepreneurship curriculum across the education system, provide opportunities for young people to be exposed to concepts and practices of entrepreneurship and enterprise development and gain early experiences with venturing. Ministries responsible for economic and SME development often work co-operatively with ministries of education to make entrepreneurship part of the core curriculum in educational institutions and fund other youth enterprise promotion programmes.

In Libya, there are some initiatives to introduce entrepreneurship in the curricula of educational programmes. The Ministry of Higher Education and the Board for Vocational Education Training have organised entrepreneurship contest conferences among students in higher education institutes. In 2013, it held the first workshop on entrepreneurial learning to discuss the means available to incorporate it into the school curriculum (OECD/EC/ETF, 2014).

In 2013, the German Corporation for International Co-operation (GIZ) conducted a review of the challenges for education and employability, surveying about 4 000 students, educators, education officials, parents and private businesses. It found that Libyan students in their final year of secondary education prefer to work in the public sector than in the private sector or in self-employment.[17] The report made a number of pertinent observations and recommendations (Box 4.6) consistent with policy and programme developments in many countries. International practices on "entrepreneurialising" all levels of the educational system, the approaches taken and lessons learned can provide useful guidance for Libya (see EACEA, 2012; OECD/EC, 2012).

Box 4.6. GIZ recommendations on educational and employability challenges of Libyan youth

The GIZ report included the following recommendations:

- Introduce entrepreneurship education and start-up training in all educational institutions, including subjects related to market analysis, management skills and business plan writing. This could be facilitated by the creation of a Libyan-Foreign Academy for Entrepreneurship.
- Develop practical entrepreneurial subjects as options for secondary school and vocational centre students.
- Introduce entrepreneurship modules in bachelor and master's degree programmes at universities.
- Improve linkages between the education sector and the labour market.
- Improve the practical business and labour market orientation of teachers, instructors and professors through training, professional development courses and company internships.
- Modernise and transform the education system to include the development of foreign languages, computer sciences, administrative and communication skills and data interpretation, plus entrepreneurial skills such as problem solving, thinking analytically, proactively and innovatively, and focusing on performance and achievement.
- Improve co-operation between private sector companies and educational institutions through regular dialogue, joint business/education projects, internship programmes for students and graduates, and teaming up with entrepreneurs to assist in teaching practical businesses processes.
- Include private sector representation in the design and implementation of reforms in the vocational training system to ensure a future orientation towards the needs of the private and SME sectors.

Source: GIZ (2013), *Libya – Building the Future with Youth: Challenges for Education and Employability.*

Notes

1. The SME programme outlined key policy areas, including establishing enterprise centres and business incubators, improving the regulatory and business environment and upgrading the legal framework, improving access to financing and creating a national network for financing and technical assistance to SMEs. It also covered building an international network to facilitate linkages with export markets and supply chains and creating infrastructure for the development of SMEs (e.g. industrial zones, technology and business parks). Finally, it set forth an entrepreneurship strategy for young people and women, adapting entrepreneurial learning and educational programmes from grade school to university and launching a communications campaign on SMEs.

2. The LPRD aims to integrate non-armed combatants into productive civilian life, either through job/skills training, further education, integration into the National Police and Army or helping them start and develop their own businesses. It is overseen by a board of directors that includes deputies of the Ministry of Labour, the Ministry of Higher Education and the Ministry of Economy. This is intended to strengthen a partnership approach and facilitate the implementation of LPRD programmes. As a member of the steering committee overseeing Libya Enterprise, the LPRD is a stakeholder in SME policy development.

3. http://sme.ly/sme/ar/.

4. For example, the Al-Jumhuriya Bank, a partially privatised, state-owned bank (accounting for 42% of the market), provides loans to SMEs and start-ups.

5. The criteria are: micro-enterprise (1-5 employees) with loans up to LYD 10 000; small enterprise (6-25 employees) with loans from LYD 10 000 –1 million; medium enterprise (26+ employees) with loans of over LYD 1 million.

6. "Libya to grant a EUR 188M loan for local SMEs", *Magharebia*, 29 July 2010 (www.animaweb.org/en/libya-grant-eur188m-loan-local-smes). The loans were intended to support 2 033 local young entrepreneurs' projects and create 5 500 new jobs.

7. The estimated portfolio of the ESDF is LYD 16 billion (about EUR 9.4 billion). Through its four holding companies, ESDF has shareholdings in about 70 local companies (majority state-owned) and several joint ventures with foreign companies. The LLIDF's initial capital was LYD 20 billion (about EUR 11.8 billion), with 75% of its equity owned by the Central Bank of Libya and the Libyan Investment Authority. The LIIDF has not been able to achieve much progress since it started its operations in 2010, committing about LYD 400 million to investment projects.

8. See "National Programme for Small and Medium Enterprises" Powerpoint slides prepared by Libya Enterprise, shared with the OECD in early 2015. The new businesses supported by the LECs indirectly created 6 530 jobs.

9. For example, retail and construction projects most probably deliver marginal social returns, while more innovative projects would carry a higher probability of impacting diversification and growth.

10. See www.ilo.org/empent/areas/start-and-improve-your-business/lang--en/index.htm/.

11. Entrepreneurship training programme of the United Nations Conference on Trade and Development (UNCTAD). See: http://empretec.unctad.org/.

12. See "Top 10 Accelerators in The Middle East and North Africa", www.wamda.com/2011/09/meet-the-top-ten-accelerators-in-mena/.

13. DfID provided funding of almost GBP 500 000. Technical assistance was obtained from SPARK, which has an international development mandate to support youth entrepreneurship in post-conflict societies (www.spark-online.org/about-us/vision-mission/).

14. www.meda.org/about-usaid-libyan-women-s-economic-empowerment.

15. This recommendation builds upon the foundation principles of the 2008 OECD Recommendation on Enhancing Integrity in Public Procurement, expanding them to reflect the critical role governance of public procurement must play in achieving efficiency and advancing public policy objectives.

16. The US defines small business as those with up to 500 workers.

17. Forty-two percent of grade 12 students would prefer to work for the government (56% of females; 39% of males). Nine percent of female students would prefer to be self-employed, compared to 14% of male students (GIZ, 2013: 47-48).

References

AfDB (2015), *Catalyzing Job Creation and Growth Through MSME Development in the Deauville Partnership Countries, Volume 2: Good Practices in Entrepreneurship Development and MSME Support*, African Development Bank, Tunis.

Commission of the European Communities (2008), "'Think Small First', A 'Small Business Act' for Europe", Communication from the Commission to the Council, the European Parliament, the European Economic and Social Committee and the Committee of the Regions, European Commission, Brussels.

CSES (Centre for Strategic and Evaluations Services (2002), "Benchmarking of Business Incubators, Final Report", European Commission, Brussels.

DfID (2013), "Strengthening Libyan Private Sector Development Support Institutions (SLPSDSI): Business Case and Intervention Summary", Department for International Development, London.

EACEA (Education, Audiovisual and Culture Executive Agency) (2012), *Entrepreneurship Education at School in Europe National Strategies, Curricula and Learning Outcomes*, European Commission, Brussels.

Expertise France, "Support to Libya for Economic Integration, Diversification and Sustainable Employment", ENPI/2014/341-913, Inception Report, Paris".

General Planning Council of Libya (2006), "Libya at the Dawn of a New Era: Improving Competitiveness in the Global Economy", General Planning Council of Libya, Tripoli.

GIZ (Deutshe Gesellschaft für Internationale Zusammenarbeit GmbH) (2013), *Libya – Building the Future with Youth: Challenges for Education and Employability*, GIZ, Bonn.

Hachmeier, K.U. (2013), "Open Government Assessment: Libya", Based on the findings of a mission to Libya, OECD, Paris.

infoDev (2010), *Global Good Practice in Incubation Policy Development and Implementation*, World Bank, Washington, DC.

KDS (Korea Institute for Development Strategy) (2010), "Establishment of SME-Oriented TVET System to Support Public Sector Reform and Employment Promotion in Libya", Korea Ministry of Strategy and Finance, Seoul.

KDS and KOREATECH (Korea University of Technology and Education) (2013), *Preparation of a Master Plan for the National Development and Implementation of Labor Market Information System for Employment Promotion in Libya*, Ministry of Strategy and Finance, Seoul.

Lewis, D.A., E. Harper-Anderson and L.A. Molnar (2011), *Incubating Success: Incubation Best Practices that Lead to Successful New Ventures*, US Department of Commerce, Washington, DC.

LIAS (Libya Institute for Advanced Studies) (2014), *Libya 2020 Vision*, Libya Institute for Advanced Studies, Tripoli.

Libya Enterprise (2015), "Budget Project, National Programme for Small and Medium Enterprises 2015", proposed budget preparation, Libya Enterprise, Tripoli.

LPRD (Libyan Programme for Reintegration and Development) (2015), "From Conflict to State-Building: Aims, Challenges and Opportunities", LPRD Progress Report 2011–2015, Libyan Programme for Reintegration and Development, Tripoli.

OECD (2015), "Recommendation on Public Procurement", http://www.oecd.org/fr/corruption/recommendation-on-public-procurement.htm.

OECD (2013), "SME and entrepreneurship financing: The role of Credit Guarantee Systems and Mutual Guarantee Societies in sustaining finance to small and medium-sized enterprises", Working Party on SMEs and Entrepreneurship (WPSMEE), Centre for Entrepreneurship, SMEs, and Local Development, OECD, Paris.

OECD (2012a), "Near Term Plan for SME Development in Libya", prepared for the Deauville Partnership with Arab Countries in Transition, October, OECD, Paris.

OECD (2012b), *Women in Business: Policies to Support Women's Entrepreneurship Development in the MENA Region*, OECD Publishing, Paris.

OECD (2008), *Enhancing the Role of SMEs in Global Value Chains*, OECD, Paris, http://dx.doi.org/10.1787/9789264051034-en.

OECD (2007), *OECD Framework for the Evaluation of SME and Entrepreneurship Policies and Programmes*, OECD, Paris.

OECD (2000), *The Bologna Charter on SME Policies.* OECD, Paris, www.oecd.org/cfe/smes/bolognaprocess.htm.

OECD and EC (European Commission) (2012), "A Guiding Framework for Entrepreneurial Universities", December, OECD, Paris.

OECD, EC and ETF (European Training Foundation) (2014), *SME Policy Index: The Mediterranean Middle East and North Africa 2014: Implementation of the "Small Business Act for Europe,* OECD Publishing, Paris.

OECD and UNIDO (United Nations Industrial Development Organisation) (2004), *Effective Policies for Small Business: A Guide for the Policy Review Process and Strategic Plans for Micro, Small and Medium Enterprise Development*, OECD, Paris.

Saadani, Y., Z. Arval and R. Rocha (2010), "A Review of Credit Guarantee Schemes in the Middle East and North Africa Region", World Bank, Washington, DC.

Schwab, K. (2014), *The Global Competitiveness Report 2014–2015*, World Economic Forum, Geneva.

The Tripoli Post (2009), *Opinion: Libya's National SME Project is re-launched.*

Transtec (2010), "Needs Assessment: Trade and Trade Related Assistance for Libya", Final report, October, European Commission, Brussels.

Upper Quartile (2013a), "Baseline M&E Data: Libyan Micro, Small and Medium Enterprises", Upper Quartile, Tripoli.

Upper Quartile (2013b), "Review of Workstream 2 – Chambers of Commerce", Libyan Private Sector Development Institutions (LPSDI), Upper Quartile, Edinburg.

VLW (2012), "National Policies on Ensuring the Economic Empowerment of Women in Libya", The Voice of Libyan Women, Zawia.

World Bank (2013), "State of Libya Financial Sector Review", World Bank, Washington, DC.

Chapter 5

Recommendations for SME policies in post-conflict Libya

This chapter provides recommendations to support SMEs and entrepreneurship in post-conflict Libya, building on the analysis of the previous chapters. There are many areas that require improvement, but policy makers should prioritise and adopt a realistic approach, paying particular attention to the sequencing of reforms. In the short term, policies should focus on rebuilding the fabric of SMEs in the country. In the longer term, it should promote economic diversification and support SMEs grow and operate in more competitive sectors. The chapter discusses the possibility of developing an SME strategy, and it includes guidance on the process.

5.1. Implications for SME policies in post-conflict Libya

In a post-conflict context in Libya, a wide range of policies will be needed to support SMEs. The government needs to foster an environment for massive entrepreneurial development in order to realise significant gains in private sector development, job creation and diversification of the productive structure.

Immediate actions should focus on rebuilding the fabric of SMEs by putting in place the necessary conditions for companies to operate. Security is essential and as long as it cannot be provided for the whole country, the government could develop safe areas from which companies could import, manufacture basic goods and provide basic services. These areas could be either temporary or they could be transformed later on into industrial areas. Another precondition to stabilise the situation should be to ensure the local and international payment system is fully operational; otherwise firms depend on their cash availability to undertake any activity. The availability of foreign currency is also essential to allow for imports, which in Libya represent a high share of basic consumption goods, and are needed as inputs for further manufacturing activities.

Medium term measures should set up and clarify the institutional framework for SME policies, defining clear roles and mandates. Key decisions should be taken regarding the level of centralisation or decentralisation of policy-making, and whether to adopt a general or a sectoral approach. In the longer term, the government can engage in more strategic and planning actions, such as diversifying the economy into priority sectors (Box 5.1), supporting SMEs accessing GVCs and become suppliers to large enterprises.

Box 5.1. **Priority sectors for diversification**

Public intervention supporting priority sectors can accelerate economic diversification, but the appropriate policies and the sequencing of reforms need to be designed carefully (IMF 2016). In order to strengthen the SME sector it is also important to open up new opportunities in diversified sectors. Training and support programmes should be put in place to build the capacity of SMEs and create a supportive environment for the entry of new entrepreneurs and businesses. Five priority sectors were identified through a sector analysis conducted in consultation with Libyan stakeholders in 2015:*

1. building and construction materials
2. agri-business
3. ICT
4. renewable energy
5. tourism/transit and trade/logistics

The final priority sectors should be selected taking into consideration the degree to which local SMEs can take advantage of opportunities in these sectors, including the ease of entry for new businesses. Sector road maps will be needed to identify the market opportunities for the sector, the specific development needs, gaps in knowledge, education and skills needs, technical limitations, infrastructure needs, market structural barriers, regulatory limitations and other barriers. The road maps should further define the concrete actions needed to address the identified gaps. Awareness of opportunities in the priority sectors will need to be created to help aspiring and existing entrepreneurs explore higher value-added activities on a sector basis.

*See section 3.1 and annex 3.1 for the full sector analysis.

Policies to support SMEs should be integrated within the broader agenda for private sector development. Framework conditions were not conducive to private sector development before 2011, and they have further deteriorated with the recent conflict. Nevertheless, previous governments did undertake significant reforms simplifying business registration, opening of new sectors to foreign investment, reducing the minimum number of shareholders in limited liability companies, introducing international standard-type legal commercial entities, reducing the corporate tax rate and liberalising trade among others.

Many new laws were introduced in 2010, but there was little time for implementation. Substantial efforts should be dedicated to support implementation of applicable legislation, including through awareness campaigns and enforcement. Contradictory laws and regulations should be harmonised. Table 5.1 summarises the institutional and legal framework of the dimensions analysed in Chapter 3. It also includes key recommendations related to these institutions and pieces of regulation. Much still needs to be done to improve the business environment in Libya. As a unity government comes to power and institutions become fully operational again, the first step should be to reassess the situation and identify what elements are valid to build on.

Table 5.1. **Summary of institutional and legal framework and key related recommendations**

Dimension	Institutions	Legal framework	Pending actions
Start-up procedures	• Libyan Commercial Register, Ministry of Economy (regional offices suspended) • Chamber of Commerce • Social Security Administration • Labour Administration • Tax Administration • Ministry of Interior • Ministry of Economy	• Commercial Law (No. 23/2010) • Civil law	• Harmonise existing regulation and undertake a communications campaign • Reopen regional offices of the business registration one-stop shop • Co-ordinate institutions involved in business start-up procedures
Land and property rights	• Real Estate Register Office (closed)	• Property Law and Real Estate registration (No. 48, 2012)	• Reopen Real Estate Register Office
Investment	• Libyan Investment Authority • Privatisation and Investment Board (PIB)	• Law on Free Zones and Transit Trade (No. 9/2000) • Law on Encouragement of Both National and Foreign Investment ("investment law") (No. 9/2010) [Replaced Law on Encouragement of Foreign Capital Investment (No. 5/1997) and Law on Promotion of Investment of Foreign Capital (No. 7/2003)] • Ministerial Decrees No. 171/2006, No. 103/2012, No. 186/2012, No. 207/2012, and No. 22/2013 (foreign participation in joint ventures)	• Amend the Investment Law to: *(a)* lift restrictions on commercial activities that currently ban foreign investors; *(b)* reduce the amount of paid-in capital required of foreign investors embarking on joint ventures with Libyan investors; and *(c)* lay down the powers of the minister of economy regarding the suspension or termination of investment projects, including the relevant legal checks controlling those powers • Harmonise laws that are currently contradictory
Trade	• Ministry of Economy	• Regional agreements: Council of Arab Economic Unity (CAEU), Greater Arab Free Trade Area (GAFTA), Arab Maghreb Union, Community of Sahel-Saharan States and the Common Market for Eastern and Southern Africa (COMESA) • Accession process to World Trade Organisation (WTO) suspended • Bilateral agreements: US-Libya Trade Agreement (2013); Framework Agreement on trade with the EU (pending)	• Resume WTO negotiations • Resume negotiations on trade agreement with the EU

Table 5.1. **Summary of institutional and legal framework and key related recommendations** *(continued)*

Dimension	Institutions	Legal framework	Pending actions
Tax regime	• Tax Registry	• Income Tax Law (No. 7/2010) • Investment Law (for foreign companies)	• Implement income tax law • Consider developing a tax regime customised to micro, small and medium enterprises (MSMEs)
Labour market	• Ministry of Labour and Manpower • Statistics Bureau • Labour Office • Libyan Board for Technical and Vocational Education (NBTVE)	• Labour Law (No. 12/2010)	• Consider revising foreign workers quotas • Develop a strategy for the employment service of job centres • Develop a comprehensive jobs strategy • Establish a labour market information system • Implement national identification number system
Financial markets	• Central Bank	• Libyan Bank Law (No. 1/2005) • Stock Market Law (No. 134/ 2007) • Law on the Securities Market (No. 11/2010) • Islamic Bank Law (No. 1/2013)	• Introduce information sharing mechanisms for lenders and investors to assess risk • Consider a dual Islamic-conventional banking system • Further develop the stock-market
Competition	• Competition Council, mandated by commercial law but to be established	• Commercial Law (No. 23/2010)	• Set up Competition Council
Innovation system	• Trademark Office, Ministry of Economy • Industrial Research Center (IRC), Ministry of Industry • Libyan Authority for Research, Science and Technology (LARST), Ministry of Higher Education and Scientific Research – Includes 33 research centres and a technology and innovation department	• Law of Intellectual Property (No. 40/1956) • Law on Patents and Industrial Designs and Models (No. 8 of 1959) • Law of Copyright Protection No. 7/1984 • Commercial Law (No. 23/2010) – Art. 1286 • National Strategy for Science, Technology and Innovation (2014)	• Implement National Strategy for Science, Technology and Innovation and link with SMEs
Infrastructure: Telecommunications	• Independent telecommunications regulatory authority (planned)	• Telecommunications Bill	• Approve telecommunications bill • Establish regulatory authority

5.2. Policy recommendations to support SMEs

Previous Libyan governments introduced several measures to support SMEs and private sector development, including programmes to provide financial assistance, support start-ups, entrepreneurship training and create a more entrepreneurial culture (Chapter 4). But many of these programmes were either put on hold or severely affected since the recent conflict in 2014. For instance, Libya Enterprise had opened five offices across the country, but by May 2016 it had regrouped its staff under its headquarters given budget constraints. Once SME policies can be relaunched, it will be useful to build on the institutions and programmes that have already been created.

In post-conflict Libya, the needs and challenges faced by SMEs will be many. SMEs in fragile and conflict affected situations particularly suffer from limited access to finance, markets, networks, and business skills (CFR, 2012). Broader economic policies will be necessary to address the biggest constraints for Libyan SMEs, such as macroeconomic and political stability (Calice et al., 2015). Vulnerable populations such as women and youth, as well as former combatants, should be paid special attention. It will be essential to involve local private sector, including SMEs, in reconstruction efforts. The government should develop measures that can support their participation, including through procurement policies and training programmes.

Libyan institutions and its partners should identify the key priorities and pay particular attention to the sequencing of measures to be implemented. Below is a broad list of recommendations to support SMEs, including some essential measures that are preconditions for any economic activity. Short term measures should focus on stabilising the system and allowing normal operations to resume. Medium term measures should aim at rebuilding the institutions and regulatory framework dealing with SME and entrepreneurship policies. In the long term, strategic action and planning can take place to develop new opportunities.

1. **Improve access to finance:** Access to finance is particularly limited in conflict environments due to lack of credit histories and business records, high collateral requirements, and insufficient financial records, and recovering the banking systems takes time. In Libya there is virtually no credit history coverage, there is no registry for movable assets, the country is in-between systems waiting to implement the Islamic or dual banking system, and inflation and the cash crisis are pushing economic activity to the informal sector. Improving access to finance should be a priority for the new government.

Short term	• Reactivate the financial sector, guaranteeing that the local and international payment system is fully functional, and ensuring the availability of foreign currency to allow for the import of essential inputs. • Implement the shift to an Islamic/dual banking system. • Reopen the Real Estate Register Office to enable registering land and property that can be used to collateralise loans.
Mid-term	• Provide training programmes for entrepreneurs to help them obtain and prepare for capital. • Clarify the banking system by stressing the supervisory role of the Central Bank, strengthening commercial banks, and bringing state banks under control of the supervisor. • Promote the development of microfinance institutions and delivery of microfinance products to start-ups and micro-enterprises. • Improve the effectiveness and flexibility of the credit guarantee system with reference to international good practices.
Long-term	• Create incentives for the establishment of a private venture capital industry. • Create a mechanism to register movable assets as collateral, either through the Real Estate Register or through a separate registry.

2. **Promote the inclusion of vulnerable population and regional balance**: Disadvantaged groups are disproportionately affected by conflict. Job creation can help demobilising militia members (Danvers, 2016). At the same time, supporting vulnerable groups can have exponential benefits. For instance, women play a critical role in post-conflict rebuilding efforts since they are often the only breadwinners left and they are more trusted in society since they tend to participate less in violent acts during war (CFR, 2012). Supporting female entrepreneurship has positive impacts at the wider household level, promotes women economic and political participation.

Short term	• Develop tailored policies targeting women and youth addressing specific constrains related to skills development, access to finance and access to networks. Alternative models such as co-operative entrepreneurship (co-operative firms, social enterprises) can be explored. • Develop programmes for population at risk such as ex-combatants and militia members. • Promote regional integration ensuring institutions, such as the business registration offices, are easily accessible beyond the capital, and work with local governments to develop SME programmes.

3. **Improve access to networks and skills, including through business development support (BDS) services**: Many entrepreneurs in conflict affected situations lack essential business skills such as the capacity to assess markets, formal accounting, record keeping, or ensuring quality standards among others. Public institutions also suffer from human capital erosion from the conflict. Capacity building and training will be essential to rebuild the Libya's SME fabric.

Short term	• Provide training and professional development programmes to build the capacity of advisors, trainers and coaches/mentors. • Assess the delivery capacity of existing enterprise centres and business incubators and impact from the conflict, and ensure they are operating.
Mid-term	• Increase the number of enterprise centres and business incubators and improve their functioning, including setting performance standards • Improve the scope and quality of LEC and incubators' services to both existing SMEs and to start-ups across a variety of topics – entrepreneurship training, productivity improvements, integrating technologies and accessing markets. • Improve the outcomes from entrepreneurship training by establishing transparent criteria for acceptance of applicants and implementing standardised and internationally-proven training materials and approaches to raise the quality and consistency of the training. • Design evaluation mechanisms to measure the impact of provided services.

4. **Improve access to markets:** Product markets are disrupted by violent events and may take time to recover. Physical infrastructure is damaged, destroyed or non-existent, becoming a main constraint for SMEs and large companies to sell their goods in domestic markets (OECD, 2012). Companies also face difficulties to improve their products to meet international standards and to get foreign customers. Countries in conflict are sometimes shut out of trade opportunities because of protectionist laws and regulations that make it difficult to export goods to international markets. Likewise, insecurity significantly affects trade, resulting in reduced access to key resources and inputs for some industries such as agricultural and livestock markets.

Short term	• Implement SME-friendly public procurement and introduce measures to support the participation of SMEs and local private sector in reconstruction projects.
Mid-term	• Develop specially designed export promotion and development programmes to develop the export potential of SMEs. This includes export readiness training; assistance in developing exportable product/ service offers; provision of information on export market opportunities; funding support for participation in foreign trade missions and exhibitions; funding support to enable SMEs to make improvements in their production processes and product quality to meet international standards; support for the formation of SME export consortia to achieve economies of scale in agri-foods, crafts and other sectors where SME activity is dominant; and provide access to export financing mechanisms. • Foster supplier development programmes to build the capacity of SMEs to act as suppliers to large firms, including technical support to bring their production and product standards into line with international standards and linkages to anchor firms. • Establish a programme to raise awareness among SMEs of opportunities of participating in global value chains (GVCs).

5. **Improve the legal and regulatory environment for start-ups and SMEs:** Weak institutional environments in fragile and conflict-affected situations have a major negative impact on the predictability of interactions with governments and other firms (Speakman and Rysova, 2015).

Short term	• Reopen the regional offices of business registration one-stop shops. • Simplify the process of registering a business and obtaining licenses and permits.
Mid-term	• Implement competition law to ensure SMEs have the opportunity to fairly compete in markets. • Create a task-force to co-ordinate reforms aimed at doing business easier.
Long-term	• Adopt the "think small first" principle advocated in the Small Business Act for Europe (Commission of the European Communities, 2008) and monitored in the SME Policy Index, which Libya participates in (OECD/EC/ETF, 2014). • Implement the guillotine regulatory review, a comprehensive approach to reviewing, streamlining, eliminating and updating regulations[1] to reduce unnecessary burden on SMEs. Normally, the guillotine process is led by a regulatory reform commission or similar entity, which Libya would have to create. • Implement a regulatory impact assessment (RIA) regime to enable an assessment of the impact on SMEs of legislative and regulatory changes as they are being proposed.

6. **Strengthen the culture of entrepreneurship:** Policies to support entrepreneurship will be particularly important in a context where public employment is the preferred option.

Mid-term	• Implement an entrepreneurship awareness campaign that includes promotion through the media and roadshows in regions, and building on other promotional activities of Libya Enterprise. • Create opportunities for Libyans to participate in workshops to learn more about entrepreneurship and the steps to take to identify business opportunities and start a business. • Organise start-up events throughout Libya, including in regions, on a regular and rotational basis. • Continue entrepreneurship competitions and the annual awards programme to celebrate entrepreneurial success.
Long-term	• Work with the Ministry of Higher Education, the Ministry of Education and the Board for Technical and Vocation Education to integrate entrepreneurship throughout the educational system. • Develop a holistic skill strategy for entrepreneurship and job creation taking into account future needs.

7. **Develop innovation and technological capacity:** In the medium and long term, it will be important to implement policies that support innovation as means to promote economic diversification.

Mid-term	• Build on existing activities that promote innovative entrepreneurs. • Make funding available to SMEs to help defray the costs of innovative activities, particularly higher-risk innovation projects, such as prototype development and commercialisation activities. • Provide support to SMEs to integrate Information and Communications Technologies (ICTs) into their business operations to improve their productivity. • Provide diagnostic consultancy services to SMEs to assess their technological capacity and readiness with follow-up technical and funding support to assist in implementation of identified opportunities.
Long-term	• Implement National Strategy for Science, Technology and Innovation and link with SMEs • Increase national awareness of the importance of innovation and entrepreneurship for economic development through promotional activities. • Facilitate linkages for SMEs with R&D support institutions, such as the Industrial Research Center and the scientific research centres under the Ministry of Higher Education and Scientific Research. • Establish innovation centres that can provide support to SMEs in solving their innovation-related challenges. • Promote the development of clusters and networks for SMEs and strengthen their links with universities and research institutions to facilitate the transfer of technology.

5.3. Developing a national SME strategy

Developing a formal SME strategy could help future governments by outlining objectives, priorities and an action plan. The strategy should be developed in consultation with the main stakeholders for SME policies. It should build on existing institutions, policies and co-ordination mechanisms while taking the opportunity to start anew and address previous deficiencies. An SME strategy should be cast within the broader agenda for private sector development.

The SME strategy would have to address two key issues. The first is reaching an agreement on an official definition of SMEs. The 2006 definition proposed by the interim General Planning Council can be a starting point. The process of deciding on a formal definition can be guided by an analysis of international practices. The second is building capacity of the Bureau of Statistics and Census to develop and implement an SME data system to address current gaps in information about the sector and to monitor developments over time. This will be essential in benchmarking Libya's annual progress in stimulating a stronger private SME sector and measuring the overall impact of SME policies and programmes.

The strategy must address the institutional setup for SME policy and co-ordination of its implementation. The establishment of a unity government will be accompanied of a restructuration of some ministries and their mandates. For instance, the Ministry of Economy and the Ministry of Industry are being merged into one. This could be taken as an opportunity to clarify the roles and mandates of institutions dealing with SME policies including the SME Policy Unit in the Ministry of Economy, Libya Enterprise, and the five regional SME funds. There needs to be a mechanism for national co-ordination of the regional approaches.

Finally, an SME strategy should include a monitoring and evaluation framework to assess the effectiveness in meeting the needs of entrepreneurs and SMEs (Box 5.2). This includes periodic reviews of its effectiveness in meeting the needs of new entrepreneurs and existing SMEs based on the collection of evaluation data and consultations with SME stakeholder groups and business support organisations (i.e. a monitoring and evaluation system to measure the impact of policies and programmes implemented as part of the strategy).

Box 5.2. Setting up a monitoring and evaluation framework for SME policies

Monitoring SME policies through client surveys can provide important information on improvements to the design and delivery of programmes. Evaluations can help assess whether the policy is correcting the problem it set out to resolve and identify whether refinements are necessary. Evaluation also assists policy makers in assessing the relative effectiveness of a portfolio of policies and programmes to determine where future efforts should be made to obtain the greatest benefit for given costs.

Given the SME Policy Unit in Libya's Ministry of Economy has a policy evaluation function, it could be involved in the design of the national SME strategy and start building its capacity to establish the appropriate evaluation mechanisms and systems. This would entail developing a system in co-operation with the Bureau of Statistics and Census for tracking annual changes in the number of SMEs (by employment size, sector, region, etc.) and their share of employment, and conducting annual SME surveys. It would also involve developing shared databases (along with demographic data) on the clients they assist for use by enterprise centres, business incubators, the credit guarantee fund, the regional SME funds, etc. Finally, it would require designing protocols to evaluate the impact on entrepreneurship/SME performance of the various forms of assistance.

Box 5.2. Setting up a monitoring and evaluation framework for SME policies *(continued)*

The process of building a monitoring and evaluation system and the related capacity is time-consuming. Technical support for the development of a proper SME data system could be requested from the OECD and Eurostat, which have expertise in this field. Libya could examine the systems in place in other MENA countries such as Algeria, Jordan and Tunisia.

Monitoring and evaluation functions should be kept separate – the SME Policy Unit should not be tasked with monitoring its own activities. For this purpose, a separate division in the Court of Auditors could be created, supervised by a public-private committee. The auditing mandate should be clear, focusing on the value-for-money of different policies and initiatives in terms of effect on the long-term structural change needed in the economy.

The process to develop an SME strategy

The process for building the national SME development strategy should be delegated to a lead government body. Depending on the government structure when the political situation is stabilised, this could be tasked to the SME Policy Unit in the Ministry of Economy in collaboration with Libya Enterprise. To steer the process, it is advisable to establish a small inter-ministerial technical committee, represented by key ministries and agencies, such as the Ministry of Economy, the Ministry of Industry, the Libyan Programme for Reintegration and Development (LPRD), the Ministry of Labour and Manpower, the Ministry of Finance, Libya Enterprise, the Chamber of Commerce and possibly the ministries responsible for education.

When formulating the national SME strategy, it will be very important for the Ministry of Economy/Libya Enterprise to consult broadly with SME stakeholders. They will need to solicit input on and validate the priority SME problems, advise on the key policy targets, objectives and strategic policy pillars, make suggestions on the lines of action to achieve objectives and targets under each policy pillar and validate the first draft of the complete strategy. This engagement of stakeholders in the work of developing the SME strategy also ensures locals buy into the elaboration and acceptance of the strategy.

Consultation meetings and focus group sessions should be held with all relevant stakeholders, including chambers of commerce and other representative business associations (including those representing women entrepreneurs). Educational institutions, other ministries, donors and donor-supported SME projects, universities and other educational/training providers, banks and relevant civil society organisations (CSOs) should also be involved.

These consultations should be held at various stages of the process: 1) at the beginning of the process to gather input on the major challenges facing entrepreneurship and SME development in the country, the key issues to be addressed in the strategy and improvements needed to the support system; 2) during the process of developing and validating the major objectives of the strategy and its overarching framework; 3) during the process of gathering input on the specific actions to realise the major objectives of the strategy; and 4) during the last stage of validating the final draft of the strategy and seeking co-operation with the relevant stakeholders on their roles and responsibilities in implementing the strategy components. The consultation sessions could take the form of one-on-one meetings, workshops, roundtables and focus groups, as appropriate.

It is very important to engage all relevant public and private sector stakeholders in the process of formulating an implementation action plan. This is critical because one of the main goals of a national SME strategy is to achieve more effective co-ordination of policy actions and a more integrated approach to delivery of SME support. Since a number of institutions may be involved in delivering SME policy measures, their engagement in the development of an action plan will be critical in facilitating the necessary level of agreement and commitment to ensure the strategy's overall success. The strategy itself would ideally lay out a five-year plan with a schedule for rolling out the various actions and programmes on an annual basis. Annual action plans would then also be prepared. Turkey recently developed a national SME strategy and can serve as example in terms of the process and the outcome (Box 5.3).

Box 5.3. Turkey's new SME strategy

SMEs play a crucial role in economic and social life in Turkey. With effective policies, well-established co-ordination among the public institutions and continuous dialogue with the private sector, the role of SMEs in the Turkish economy has grown dramatically in recent years. There are more than 3.5 million SMEs in the country, employing 76% of the workforce and accounting for nearly 63% of enterprise turnover, more than 50% of value added and 60% of exports. SMEs are defined as enterprises with fewer than 250 employees whose annual net turnover or annual balance sheet is under TL 40 million.

To better support SMEs, Turkey developed its second national strategy, the "SME Strategy and Action Plan (2015-2018)", under the leadership of the Turkish Small and Medium Enterprises Development Organisation (KOSGEB).

The process: Developing a national SME strategy

Developing the SME Strategy entailed four stages: 1) define the general purpose of the strategy; 2) agree on the strategic areas; 3) determine the strategic targets; and 4) decide on the actions to reach the targets.

To arrive at the general purpose statement, KOSGEB first formed two high-level committees, one at the ministerial level and one at the deputy-secretary level. The two committees held a two-day meeting with 200 representatives from different stakeholder organisations to generate the general purpose statement. The second stage entailed a consultative process with diverse stakeholders to confirm the strategic areas of policy focus for the strategy.

Once the strategic areas were determined, KOSGEB established five expert groups, each one assigned to a strategic area and tasked with defining the targets for that area. Following this stage, the expert groups outlined the actions to be taken to realise the targets. All relevant stakeholder organisations in Turkey (e.g. other government organisations, universities, unions, business associations, etc.) were given a role in defining actions, as in many cases, they would end up responsible for their implementation. When the strategy was drafted, it was presented to the ministerial council for approval and became an official government document.

A steering committee was formed to monitor progress on implementation of the four-year strategy. All institutions responsible for implementing actions are required to report to KOSGEB on the progress made on their action plan commitments. Twice a year, the steering committee brings together all relevant stakeholders to review what has been done and to gather feedback. A semi-annual report on the progress is submitted to the higher-level committee.

Box 5.3. **Turkey's new SME strategy** *(continued)*

The outcome: Turkey's SME development policy framework and support programmes

A number of government agencies are involved in implementing effective policies and programmes to address barriers to the increased competitiveness of SMEs and the SME sector, including the Ministry of Science, Industry and Technology, the Small and Medium Enterprises Development Organisation (KOSGEB), the Scientific and Technological Research Council and the Regional Development Agencies. KOSGEB, established in 1990, is the main body for executing the policies regulating SMEs. Its main purpose is to increase the share and effectiveness of SMEs in the economy, raise their competitiveness and realise their greater integration in economic development. KOSGEB carries out a variety of programmes to support SMEs through 88 branches in 81 cities across Turkey. In the past ten years, more than USD 1 billion has been allocated to SME development through eight different support programmes. Almost 800 000 SMEs are registered in the KOSGEB database.

The first challenge in developing a policy framework for SME development in Turkey was agreeing to a common definition of SMEs. Prior to 2008, a number of definitions were in use by different agencies, which caused problems. In 2008, a cabinet decision harmonised the definition to be consistent with the European Union definition: an SME has fewer than 250 workers or less than USD 15 million in turnover.

The goal of the SME Strategy and Action Plan (2015-18) is to increase the contribution of SMEs to national economic growth and international competitiveness. The strategic targets for the action plan are as follows: a) increase SME exports to USD 150 billion; b) increase the number of exporting SMEs to 60 000; c) maintain SMEs' commercial R&D expenses at 33%; and d) create 3 million new jobs in SMEs.

The five strategic areas defined in the SME Strategy and action plan are the following:

1. improving and supporting entrepreneurship
2. improving SMEs' capability and business management skills
3. supporting SMEs through improvements to the business and investment environment
4. improving SMEs' R&D and innovation capacity
5. facilitating access of SMEs and entrepreneurs to financing.

The Entrepreneurship Support Programme was created to disseminate a culture of entrepreneurship. It consists of a number of sub-programmes: the Entrepreneurship Training Programme, the New Entrepreneurs Support (financing for new start-ups – TL 30 000 of grant funding and TL 70 000 in repayable loans) and the Business Incubator Support Programme. Subsidies of 80% are available to fund the business plans developed by potential entrepreneurs completing the training, who can then develop their start-up in one of the business incubators. To date, 335 000 entrepreneurs have been trained, of which nearly 20 000 started businesses from the 19 business incubators.

The R&D, Innovation and Industrial Implementation Programme provides support to SMEs and entrepreneurs in developing new ideas and inventions and engaging in innovative activities of SMEs. The focus of this programme is supporting R&D projects that provide value added of up to USD 600 000. Universities are a strong partner in delivering this programme support, including in some cases by establishing technology incubators.

Most SMEs in Turkey are micro-enterprises, so the policy framework reflects the need to help micro-enterprises become larger and reach competitive scale. KOSGEB promotes micro-enterprise clusters to facilitate collaboration, such as through common purchasing to reduce input costs, equipment sharing and formation of design and marketing consortia. For these purposes, micro-enterprises are encouraged to mobilise in groups of three to five to collaborate on joint projects.

Box 5.3. **Turkey's new SME strategy** *(continued)*

The General Support Programme is geared towards developing the capacity of SMEs to develop projects in target sectors, which includes improving their marketing activities to expand their share of domestic and international markets. It also covers support for employment of qualified staff, consultancy, energy efficiency, foreign business travel, business matching, etc. The Thematic Project Support Programme aims to meet the regional and sectoral needs of the country by taking into account these priorities in support to SMEs.

Access to finance is a perennial SME policy issue. Following the 2008-2009 financial crisis, during which Turkish SMEs were hit hard, the government implemented reforms to address their liquidity and working capital constraints and make bank financing more feasible for them. KOSGEB's Credit Interest Support Programme covers the loan interest on bank loans to eligible SMEs. More than 215 000 SMEs have benefited from this support, using credits from 17 banks with which KOSGEB has signed protocols. With this support, SMEs have been able to access a total credit volume of USD 7 billion since 2008. The Credit Guarantee Fund is another policy tool to help address the collateral constraints facing SMEs who need bank financing. On the equity side, which is critical for high-technology start-ups and growth-oriented SMEs, the government funded a Fund of Funds to provide an investment incentive for private equity and venture capital funds. Given that SMEs were not able to take advantage of capital markets to accelerate their growth, the Turkey Stock Exchange developed the secondary market for emerging companies. KOSGEB designed the Emerging Enterprises Market Programme to support the entry of growth-potential SMEs in the secondary market subsidising consultancy fees to support SMEs in meeting the listing requirements.

Source: Presentation of S.Tuna ŞAHİN, vice-president, Small and Medium Enterprises Development Organization (KOSGEB), Turkey, at the OECD meeting "SME Development Strategy Project for Libya: Consultative meeting for the diagnostic study", 29-30 July 2015, Istanbul.

Note

1. The Regulatory Guillotine™ (Jacobs, 2006) process counts the existing regulations and then reviews each one against clear criteria, using an orderly and transparent method built on extensive stakeholder input. It provides both a quick fix to the most critical problems of inefficient and anti-market regulations, and a permanent system for quality control of new business regulations to avoid re-occurrence of the same problems. It is a flexible method specifically designed through a precise sequence to produce good results even where resistance is high.

References

Calice, P., et al. (2015), *Simplified Enterprise Survey and Private Sector Mapping: Libya 2015*, World Bank Group, Washington, DC, http://documents.worldbank.org/curated/en/2015/09/25016718/simplified-enterprise-survey-private-sector-mapping-libya-2015.

CFR (2012), "Entrepreneurship in Post-conflict Zones", Working Paper, Council on Foreign Relations, Washington, DC, www.cfr.org/entrepreneurship/entrepreneurship-postconflict-zones/p28257.

Danvers, William (2016), "Next Steps in Libya: Economic and Governance Stabilization in the Face of Political and Security Challenges", Center for American Progress, Washington, DC.

IMF (2016), "Economic Diversification in Oil-Exporting Arab Countries", Annual Meeting of Arab Ministers of Finance.

Jacobs, S. (2006), "Effective and Sustainable Regulatory Reform: The Regulatory Guillotine in Three Transition and Developing Countries", Jacobs and Associates, Washington, DC, http://regulatoryreform.com/wp-content/uploads/2015/02/Evaluation_of_the_regulatory_guillotine_in_7_countries_2006.pdf.

OECD (2012), "Empowerment in fragile states and situations of fragility", OECD Publishing, Paris, http://dx.doi.org/10.1787/9789264168350-8-en.

Speakman, John and Annoula Rysova (2015), *The Small Entrepreneur in Fragile and Conflict-Affected Situations*, World Bank, Washington, DC.

ORGANISATION FOR ECONOMIC CO-OPERATION AND DEVELOPMENT

The OECD is a unique forum where governments work together to address the economic, social and environmental challenges of globalisation. The OECD is also at the forefront of efforts to understand and to help governments respond to new developments and concerns, such as corporate governance, the information economy and the challenges of an ageing population. The Organisation provides a setting where governments can compare policy experiences, seek answers to common problems, identify good practice and work to co-ordinate domestic and international policies.

The OECD member countries are: Australia, Austria, Belgium, Canada, Chile, the Czech Republic, Denmark, Estonia, Finland, France, Germany, Greece, Hungary, Iceland, Ireland, Israel, Italy, Japan, Korea, Latvia, Luxembourg, Mexico, the Netherlands, New Zealand, Norway, Poland, Portugal, the Slovak Republic, Slovenia, Spain, Sweden, Switzerland, Turkey, the United Kingdom and the United States. The European Union takes part in the work of the OECD.

OECD Publishing disseminates widely the results of the Organisation's statistics gathering and research on economic, social and environmental issues, as well as the conventions, guidelines and standards agreed by its members.

OECD PUBLISHING, 2, rue André-Pascal, 75775 PARIS CEDEX 16
(03 2016 11 1 P) ISBN 978-92-64-26419-9 – 2016

www.ingramcontent.com/pod-product-compliance
Ingram Content Group UK Ltd.
Pitfield, Milton Keynes, MK11 3LW, UK
UKHW051241300926
15471UKWH00015B/1451

9 789264 264199